30-Days

To Clarity, Communion, & A Closer Connection with God in A Chaotic World

Lakisha Shaffer

motique media

Publishing division of Motique Momentums, LLC

www.danielaGabrielle.com

ISBN:069241682x
ISBN-13:9780692416822

DEDICATION

To my AMAZING family!

I thank God for my awesome children and wonderful husband Fred. You made time for me to pursue my dreams and provided the encouragement I needed every step of the way. I could not have done this without the Shaffer family.

Fred, you were such a encouragement throughout this whole process. I want to say thank you and I love you with all my heart. I thank God for you- the leader of my household. I love the way you nurture, not only our children, but me as well. You're a great provider both physically and spiritually. You provide the environment for our household to thrive. Thank you for being a praying man and a strong tower in Christ. I love you so much!

To my parents, William and Joyce. Thank you for allowing me the opportunity to grow up and be taught the ways of the Lord. You have helped me throughout the years to be a strong Christian wife and mother who's never afraid to show my faith. I love you both and I thank God for you.

To my spiritual leaders, thank you for speaking the Word of God to me and walking out the word in front of me. I thank God for the work that you do and the way that you allow the Lord to use you as a vessel for him. Continue to shine a light down the path to God for all to follow.

Last, but not least I want to thank God for how awesome and wonderful he is to me! God, you are the air that I breathe, the lover of my soul, and my Prince of Peace. I love you for everything you've done and will continually to do for me and my family.

I love you for loving me enough and choosing me to be one of your children. You are my everything and I love you in every way.

CONTENTS

INTRODUCTION

Life has its way of consuming your thoughts, your mind, your actions, and your souls without one recognizing it. **Let's start here...**

Take a moment and close your eyes.

> What's on your mind?
>
> Are your thoughts racing?
>
> Are you feeling emotional about something that happened during the day?
>
> Are you even able to focus enough to discern what's on your mind?

Ahhhhh...life, with so many distractions and things pulling on you, the noise of the world is constantly competing for your attention. It often makes it hard to know and seek after your true desires and God's will for your life.

Now imagine being able to at anytime of the day, press pause and tune into God during those moments of chaos. Can you image closing the eyes of your mind and allowing God unlimited access to shine light to any area that may be in need of renewal from the stress of life? That level of peace is available and it comes as you master the art of pressing pause.

As you prepare for this journey ask God to show you the things that are in your heart, life, and character that you need to deal with. Allow this to be a time where you mature through a season of healing and letting go. You'll soon have an extraordinary key that will benefit you in every area of your life.

The ability to personally reflect with God on a daily basis will help you unlock personal insight and unlimited potential while re-creating and re-building your character.

Self-reflection with God is the ability to look beyond your actions to explore the root or cause of those actions. Oftentimes, people only look at the surface, but when you choose self-reflection with God you are able to get a "God-glimpse" of your character in conjunction with your motives. In that place with God, you are able to understand your actions and receive clarity on how to find freedom in Him.

Self-reflection is not an easy thing for most people to do. It is an intentional journey that requires commitment to get to the root of the issues in your life. It's not easy to be transparent about where you are in life. It takes courage to confront yourself and a lot of guts to actually sit down and actively work on what you see. Here's the reality, you are strong enough to face the man in the mirror and when you do, you will reach your full potential in life.

To experience the fullness of your Press Pause experience, be willing to ask yourself the difficult questions.

> What is the real reason I'm doing this?
>
> Do I really feel this way about the situation?
>
> Do I really want to resolve this conflict?
>
> What is really keeping me from spending time with God?
>
> Do I really want to forgive?

Asking these types of questions and answering them honestly will uncover how you truly feel about life's issues. It positions you to no longer Band-Aid areas of your life that need your attention.

Asking the difficult questions reveals your

inner thoughts, underlying hurts, true feelings, as well as unfinished or wounded areas in your life. It forces you to look at yourself through the light of God. The more you do this, the more you get to know yourself. The brilliant part about learning to Press Pause is that time of reflecting with God forces you to tackle the unconscious hidden agendas that sabotage your full potential.

What is Press Pause all about? It's about creating opportunities to press pause, get into the presence of God, and personally reflect on life and the world around you. It is a significant time of surrendering your heart to God while you reflect on what He shows you. During these moments, God will shine light on the areas that have been neglected, grown dim over time, and have become dark.

You will draw near to God's light as you learn to Press Pause. Letting God shine light in your heart, will draw the things you desire. It will revive old dreams, stir abandoned ambitions and restore broken promises. In these times of drawing near, God will shine light on situations and solutions that do not exist and those answers will allow you to move forward.

Prepare you heart for this journey to break through in the darkest, hardest, and more challenging places of your life. Posture yourself for the transformation of a lifetime as you learn to Press Pause.

Living The Press Pause Lifestyle

Over the next thirty-days you will journey to live a Press Pause lifestyle. There are two ways to implement this lifestyle into your daily routine.

THE *MORNING PAUSE*

Rise and shine by experiencing the light of a morning pause. Pressing pause before starting your day will make room for communion and deep connection with God to hear from him concerning your day. Learning to make God's voice the first thing you hear each day, makes room for a more intimate listening and responding relationship with God. The more you engage in the morning pause, the more likely you are for this to become a habit. Every morning pause opens you to God before starting your day and you'll be in tune with the leadings of His spirit and the things on God's heart.

YOUR *MORNING PAUSE* IMPLEMENTATION STRATEGY

Start as soon as your eyes open. Press Pause by taking a few moments to thank God for the day.

Hang out with God. Spend two or three minutes with Him before you actually get out of bed.

Have a sweet spot. Identify a *secret place* where you can spend some uninterrupted time with God. This place can be a home office, spare bedroom, closet, your car, or even a quiet corner in your living room. Wherever that place is, that's where we'll spend a little time sitting down with God in our heart.

Ask for a reflection encounter. Ask God to reflect on our heart, the things that He wants to bring to the light for you to work on. Ask Him for a Devine encounter where He shows you where to focus for the day.

Dive deep into the solutions from God's word. Once you have an idea of where God wants to focus, take a few minutes to get into God's word on any subject, incident, situation, habit, or mindset that He wants you to work on. Use your Journal to write out the things that God reveals to you during this time. Find scriptures that will help you to see God's heart and what His word says about what He's revealed to you.

Take your encounter with you. Before you jump up to start your day, be sure to jot down one or two scriptures from your Morning Pause on an index card. Tuck that card in your pocket or purse and meditate on it throughout the day.

THE *MORNING PAUSE* SECRET

The morning pause positions you to hear from your Creator. By giving God your morning, you position yourself to deal with areas that may not be so obvious to identify. As your Creator, He knows the secrets of your heart and holds the power to transform you to experience a prosperous life spiritually, emotionally and physically.

PRESS PAUSE MOMENTS

Press Pause moments are practical ways to acknowledge situations, circumstances, troubles, or problems that need our immediate attention, reaction, or response throughout our day. The truth about life is that challenges are always around. How you respond determines the impact of those challenges on your life.

You know that things change from morning to evening; Press Pause moments help you take a second, press pause, and seek God for His wisdom on how to correctly handle what is before you. As you adapt this lifestyle, you'll learn how to move forward with Christ and when things arise in your day that may be difficult, you'll have the tools necessary to move forward gracefully.

YOUR *PRESS PAUSE MOMENTS* IMPLEMENTATION STRATEGY

Look for opportunities to press pause. As you go throughout your day, ask God to help you be aware of *press pause moments*. As He makes you aware, it will help you take the timeout that you need to get his heart on whatever you're facing before your response, emotions, or feelings get involved.

Get a fresh perspective in the moment. Reflect on God, how He is, and what His word says in your situation. This will help you to respond to life's circumstances out of love and from a place of wholeness.

Let the moment plant a fresh perspective. As you press pause throughout your day, God plants new seeds of wisdom to address life's occurrences. Those seeds will become strongly rooted seeds that flourish and bring forth good fruit in your lives.

PRESS PAUSE MUST-HAVE KIT

- Holy Bible (King James, NIV, Amplified, study Bible)
- (Press Pause) Journal
- At least 2 pens or pencils
- Highlighter
- Index cards
- Index card holder
- Worship music

Suggestions: *Fred Hammond, Kari Jobe, James Eddie, Hillsong, Chris Tomlinson, Israel and New Breed*

- A desire for more intimacy with God
- A desire to embrace a life of character building
- A desire to get to know yourself in a deeper level with the help of God

You will need your favorite study Bible to get into the Word and study the Scriptures that are given daily. Your journal will give you a dedicated place to write down any insight that God gives you about yourself. You want a journal also to gain a day-to-day look at your progress. It will also help you pinpoint any areas that you see God revealing on a daily basis.

You highlighter will allow you to highlight passages that God may point out to you in the Bible to reflect on. It will help those words to be illuminated and stand out as we study the Word in the future.

Writing out the scriptures that God gives you along the journey will allow you to reflect and meditate on the areas that God wants to transform. Documenting them on index cards so you can put the scriptures in a little cardholder, will make the scriptures handier to pull out when needed during prayer and worship.

Commonly Used Symbols or Expressions

▶**Press Play:** is when a story, scenario, or point is being made about something

(| |) Press Pause: to take a look at, step back from, or a teachable moment

⇦**Press Rewind**: to go over something or to revisit a place, feeling or emotion

⇨**Fast forward**: to move ahead and look to God

PRESS PAUSE: PERSONAL REFLECTION

DAY ONE

SIT DOWN WITH GOD IN YOUR HEART

"...Love the Lord your God with all your heart and with all your soul and with all your mind". Matt.22: 37 KJV

There are a lot of things that God wants you to have and get out of life. He wants you to enjoy an abundant life in Him. Position yourself to be open and transparent before the Lord, allowing Him into all parts of your life today. God wants your heart and this is the starting place, the center that will encourage healing, restoration, and blessings for the rest of your body.

God desires that you walk through this life whole and healthy. He desires good things for you. Not just material things, but spiritual things as well. I challenge you to give God your whole heart and allow him to make your heart whole. As you do, His desire for you to walk in love, peace, joy, strength, happiness and have a full life will begin to manifest.

Today as you sit with God, seek Him with your whole heart. Don't ask for things from your own agenda, but instead ask Him to infuse His heart for your life into your heart so that your desires begin to align with His. You gain that which the Lord desires for you to have, by diving into the word of God, seeking his heart, and asking for understanding.

Trust that God knows best.

As you go through your day, choose not to lean on your own understanding, but on His wisdom and knowledge. Every moment that you need to move forward, make a conscious decision to ask God to lead and guide you. As you allow Him to take the lead, starting with your heart, you make a pathway to see your true self, unfiltered and unhindered by your own views or expectations.

Let us allow God to shower his love on us as he walks and talks with us today. Let's stay open to the Holy Spirit allowing him to lead and guide us throughout our week. Let's make our time with God special and allow his spirit to bring the peace and wholeness we need in our hearts.

Before you start your day, take a moment to PRESS PAUSE and ask yourself some questions while reflecting on what you read today. Record your responses and hold yourself accountable to walking these responses out on your journey.

In what way can you make time and space in your schedule to spend with God each day?

____

____

____

____

____

____

____

Are you ready and willing to open up all of the areas in your life to receive the love and change needed that God will provide? Why or why not?

____

____

____

Are you ready to accelerate your spiritual maturity and see all the blessings and glory that getting close with God can bring into your life?

- o Yes
- o No

Do you believe that God wants your whole heart?

- o Yes
- o No

Write out two examples of what your heart and life would look like whole. Imagine yourself free from your past hurts, limitations, and obstacles.

EXAMPLE ONE

____

____

____

____

____

____

____

EXAMPLE TWO

____

____

____

____

____

____

____

What are three steps that YOU can take to begin to bring your heart to a place of wholeness?

STEP ONE

____

____

____

STEP TWO

____

____

____

STEP THREE

____

____

____

⇨**Fast forward:** Father God, give me the grace and strength to give you my heart so that you can make it whole. Give me the strategy to make time for you and the courage to open up my heart so that you can do the work that is needed in my life. Thank you for your love, grace, and mercy.

In Jesus' name,

Amen.

DAY TWO

WHAT'S IN YOUR HEART

"The precepts of the LORD are right, giving joy to the heart. The commands of the LORD are radiant, giving light to the eyes." Psalms 19:8 KJV

Do you ever catch yourself being upset about a certain thing or person at times? Have you ever instantly caught an attitude that felt seemingly out of nowhere and you couldn't pinpoint exactly why? Have you ever been somewhere and were overcome with emotion, barely able to control yourself out of the blue and had no real clue the source of those feelings? Can you think back to any time in your life that you prejudged a person or situation, only to find out later that it was nothing even close to what you assumed or judged it to be? What about a time last month that you felt disrespected and you weren't sure exactly where the disrespect came from, but the disrespect felt very real? What about even a time that you didn't feel like yourself and you struggled to put yourself together?

You are not alone in this chaotic ocean of emotions and perceptions. The truth is everyone faces moments like these, but what if what you discovered that those common moments might not be so common or harmless after all? The key is learning how to filter what life brings you and be open to God filling your heart with a reasonable solution to overcome them. In the midst of all of those emotions, are clues to broken pieces in your heart that need to be uncovered and addressed.

Now that you've drummed up some things that are unsettling in your own life, think back over them and start reflecting. I will demonstrate the manifestation of a fragmented heart as an example of what I really mean.

Start with: Catching an attitude seemingly out of nowhere

▶**Press Play:** I remember one day being tired and feeling like I wasn't getting a lot done around the house. I felt fine to myself, just a slight hint of frustration, but nothing I couldn't handle. So as I'm going around the house cleaning and doing some daily chores, I began to imagine how much easier my life would be if my kids would put their stuff away. I mean really! They're old enough to at least put their cereal bowls away when they're done eating; that couldn't possibly be too much to ask, could it? And if only my husband would back me up with the kids doing the little bit of chores that we asked them to do. You know the conversation, you've had it before- *or one similar.*

Shortly after, my husband comes home and asks, "How was your day?" He even goes on to compliment me on how nice I look today. I should be blushing by now, right? Not!

Instead I'm instantly irritated and here goes that inner conversation again. "I mean I'm running around here picking up after everybody. I'm tired and didn't really take any time out to do anything INCLUDING combing my hair. Uggggggh! I don't even know if my clothes are matching at this point AND he has the NERVE to comment on how nice I look today. He has got to be kidding. Does he know that I had to pick up after the kids from where they spilled cereal on table and oh yea, did I mention that they totally missed the garbage when pouring it out so I had to scrub the walls next to the garbage can too, but yet I look NICE today?

(| |) Press Pause: I take a deep breath to gather myself and go into my home office (my secret place). I sit there for a minute and reflect on why I REALLY feel so irritated. I asked the Lord to show me what's going on with my attitude. The first thing he shows me is that there's not a problem with my attitude there's an underlying issue in my heart. My frustration had nothing to do with what my husband said or anything else going on at that present time. It had to do with what was already in my heart.

The truth was, I let frustration build up over time. It wasn't the first time that things were out of place at home. Life happens! Things happen! But when you only focus on the outside frustrations you miss what's going on with YOU.

I was frustrated because I chose not to check my feelings at the door, instantly press pause, and reflect on how I felt at the first sign of discontentment. Now the result of not doing that early on had led to me to being so irritated that even a nice word and compliment couldn't bless me.

When you press pause at the first sign of adversity or discontentment you make room for God to show you how and what to do in a particular situation. It helps you do things more thoroughly and in graceful and godly manner.

When things build up in your heart over days, months, years or even decades, it blurs our judgment and reasoning through different situations. During those times it's hard to see things as black and white or right or wrong, because your vision is not clear to see the situation for what it is.

Unfinished or unresolved issues in your heart become the foundation of your reactions, thought processes, mannerisms, and your decisions. The hurt and wounds of life can create the misguidance of your heart. That's why it is essential for you to live a press pause lifestyle of reflection. To help you to bring truth to the decisions in your daily lives.

A PRESS PAUSE lifestyle will help you keep a better guard over your heart. You want to keep your heart clean, clear, and healthy so that as you live out your days, you can judge things more effectively because you are living and speaking from a place that is whole.

"Above all else, guard your heart, for everything you do flows from it." *Proverbs 4:23*

As you reflect daily, this PRESS PAUSE lifestyle can catapult you by leaps and bounds in your spiritual walk. It is a major key to spiritual growth and maturity. If you respond in a more appropriate way when challenged with trials, problems, and tests, you will drastically change the course of your life.

⇨**Fast forward:** Father I thank you for helping me keep a guard around my heart. As I grow spiritually, allow me to respond out of your heart and see situations from your perspective. I thank you that my heart and mind are being renewed daily by your word.

In Jesus' name,

Amen.

Before you start your day, take a moment to PRESS PAUSE and ask yourself some questions while reflecting on what you read today. Record your responses and hold yourself accountable to walking these responses out on your journey.

Think back on a recent time that you reacted from a broken place. How would that have gone differently had you known to PRESS PAUSE with God?

____

____

____

____

____

____

____

Name two positive results that you would have gained by pressing pause in that situation?

RESULT ONE

____

____

____

RESULT TWO

____

____

____

What is one thing that you would do differently if faced with a similar situation in the future?

____

____

____

What two ways can you see yourself benefiting from by being able to PRESS PAUSE with issues of your heart immediately?

BENEFIT ONE

____

____

____

BENEFIT TWO

____

____

____

What is a practical technique that you can implement to help you guard your heart in the future?

____

____

____

⇨**Fast Forward:** Father God, as I sit here before you with my eyes closed, my mind clear, and my heart open, I ask you to search the depths of my heart and bring to light the areas that I have overlooked and neglected in the past. I ask that, as I start the journey of pressing pause by spending time with you, you would help me to rebuild a strong foundation within my heart with the divine pieces that you will put there for me to live and have a healthy whole heart.

Father God, I ask that as I start this journey and spend time sitting down with you in my heart that you would touch every fiber of my being. I ask that you would give me the keys to totally and wholly deal with the issues of my heart. I ask you to search my heart for the things that you want to shed light on. Father, I ask that as you shine your light on these areas that I would be able to connect with your heart on these issues. Let me be open to change in these areas fully and completely to live out my full potential of your will for my life. I open my heart to you. I love you and fully trust your guidance.

In Jesus' name,

Amen

DAY THREE

PRESS PAUSE ON YOUR FEELINGS

"My grace is sufficient for you, for my power is made perfect in weakness."

2 Corinthians 12:9 KJV

It's not always about who has done something TO you or what was said ABOUT you, moreover it's not even about how YOU felt or YOUR feelings in the moment. Life's situations are about how you RESPOND. It is how you interpret these situations and the way you allow it to affect change in your life.

Declare this, ***"It's not about them, it's about ME! I have the POWER to choose my response"***

Do you find yourself making or changing your decisions based on how you feel from day to day?

Oftentimes people allow their feelings to guide their decision-making. The problem with this is that your feelings are not always trustworthy. The seat of your emotions is rooted in you heart and your heart carries life's issues. Therefore, while you may want to always follow your feelings, they can sometimes come from an unfinished place that's wounded, hurt, dissatisfied or altered due to unresolved issues. Living a PRESS PAUSE lifestyle with God at the helm to guide helps you to take that needed time-out in moments of adversity, frustration, dissatisfaction and discontentment.

By doing this, pressing pause allows you to step back from what's presented and look at the situation without the misguiding of your feelings. See, feelings are fickle, they like to pull up past or similar experiences. Then, they add irrelevant feelings to go along with a situation in your life. The joy of pressing pause is that you can separate those emotions from your situation and examine what you're facing using the facts and wisdom from God which allows you to make better decisions. Pressing pause gives you the ability to think clearer and react in a more effective way.

Can you imagine how peaceful your life will be when you're not living on "ten" or *"feeling some type of way"* all the time? A PRESS PAUSE lifestyle promotes and promises ***peace***!

▶ **Press Play:** A few years ago I found myself completely frustrated with my living situation. My husband and I were newly married, we had just bought our first house and we allowed a family member to move into the other apartment. Things are good for a while, but soon I began to feel discontent with the arrangement. We had a small family and they had a small family. Although there were two separate units, I started to notice a few blurred lines. The families would often go back and forth to both apartments, which weren't major problems, but sometimes they would get into food that I was preparing for dinner or taking to an event at church. As time went on other issues began to pop up like our doors not being locked after finishing laundry or me cooking for both families three to four times a week to accommodate the schedules of both households.

Of course when you have two families in such close quarters there's also the difference in the way the children are raised and the joys of random things around the house getting broken. To add to the situation, there was also the addition of more family guests and then here comes the secret conversations that start to stir feelings of division and animosity. If you haven't lived this story, I'm sure in your lifetime, you have heard some version of it. You step into a good deed, forget to set boundaries, and end up becoming the "bitter one." Now everyone's looking at you like YOU'RE crazy and you're secretly looking at him or her like LEAVE NOW!

Can you relate?

Obviously this arrangement led to some disagreements in my relationship with my husband and as time went on I began to feel uncomfortable in my own home. I noticed myself wanting to visit with friends and family more often when the truth was I was truly tired and wished I could just go to MY home and rest. Feeling this way only drew out what was in my heart. Before I knew it I was starting to become snappy, frustrated and withdrawn, which was no way for newlyweds to start a marriage.

As I faced my truth, I knew there had to be a change. It was time for us to grow as a newly married couple on our own and to begin building our new family together. Facing my truth positioned me to look for solutions with God instead of harboring discontentment in my heart.

Press Rewind: Let's examine MY feelings. I felt like they were the problem, I felt like they were violating my home and I felt worse, because no one could understand my silent frustration. In my head, they should've known why I was snappy. They should get it! Why couldn't they get it? But here's the truth again, we grew up two entirely different ways.

Growing up in my household, if you bought something you put your name on it or if it's in your refrigerator, it's yours and no one else should touch it. The way my husband was brought up, if it's in the refrigerator and someone wants it they can have it. The truth was, we were all drawing from our own separate set of experiences and being out numbered, there was no one drawing from my well. That's why my feelings were moving in a direction so distinctively different from everyone else's.

(| |) Press Pause: One night I am talking to a friend about a situation she was going through. As we are talking I could clearly see how she was allowing the situation to control her feelings and her emotions. It was obvious that she was being unrealistic with her perception of the situation from the outside looking in and it was my job to help her see it from another point of view. It's easy to see things clearly when you are not in the situation. So as an impartial party in the matter I go on to tell her that, "Regardless of what someone is doing or has done, you still have a choice of how you react to it." High five Lakisha! That's some good stuff. I go on to tell her how in my own life I don't allow everything that is brought before me to shake me as a person. I was like, "Girl, I will dismiss something like what you're going through, before I ever let it control my life!" High five again Lakisha, I was on a roll!

You know where I'm going next, *right*?

Now as I'm talking to my friend dishing out all this good wisdom and revelation, the Holy Spirit stirs up and boom...allows me to pause and listen to myself as I'm helping my friend. That small still comforter urged me to look at my own situation in the same manner and with the same restraints I was asking her to do.

It wasn't until I paused, took my feelings out of the equation, and then looked at the situation differently that I was able to find the path to a better place in my situation. With the wisdom that came from that PRESS PAUSE moment, I was able to share my feelings, set boundaries, and become up front about the things that had to change. We were able to gain a mutual respect for our differences, which made everything in the home run a lot smoother.

Our community home life began to become a lot of fun as we worked things out. It even brought us closer together as an immediate and extended family. Eventually they did buy their own place and move on, but in the process we established a long lasting life-giving relationship.

Things didn't transform overnight. Navigating the situation was a process, but I made a choice to change my perception, which changed my attitude. I reflected on God and instead of asking Him to take me out of it, I asked him to show me how to walk through it and how to see the situation through his eyes.

During this time I learned a lot. I learned that

even as an already patient person, I could become more patient. I discovered that differences were actually okay and that if I address things early on I could avoid tons of stress. Through what felt like a tough time, I learned how to abound in love as well as extend and receive grace.

As a result of my Press Pause lifestyle, I was able to hold onto and continue a strong healthy relationship with my family members. When I pressed pause, I saw the beauty of it all for both families. A family was able to get back on its feet and I was able gain a new perspective on life by having them around. The truth was that what felt uncomfortable, was actually a win for us all and I would have never understood that without pressing pause.

Life will bring you trials, but before you run to ask God to take it away, PRESS PAUSE and experience the benefit of navigating the problem with God. Here's your truth, "It's more important that you learn how to deal with things in a true and honest way, so that you prosper regardless of if God takes it away." Not only can you get through it, you can get through it with grace and walk away having matured spiritually.

Before you start your day, take a moment to PRESS PAUSE and ask yourself some questions while reflecting on what you read today. Record your responses and hold yourself accountable to walking these responses out on your journey.

How often have you let your feelings guide your decision-making?

____

____

____

____

____

____

____

____

____

____

____

____

Have your feelings ever gotten in the way of you seeing the beauty in a situation that actually turned out to bless your life?

____

____

____

____

____

____

____

What are two steps you can take to press pause and get God's perspective on a situation you're dealing with in your feelings right now?

____

____

____

____

____

____

____

What technique will you implement to help you separate your feelings from facts?

Thoughts & Reflections:

⇨**Fast Forward:** Thank you Father for knowing me better than I know myself. Thank you for helping me see past my own thoughts and feelings and see others and myself in the way that you see us. Father, today I open my heart and feelings to you. I give you permission to help me refrain from moving through life wrapped up in my feelings and responding to things unrealistically due to my own issues. Help me to focus on you and your ways. Let my responses in life align with you and your Word.

I thank you Father, because you are faithful to show me my rights and my wrongs. Help me not to ignore your small still voice directing me, but let me be sensitive to your guidance. I love you for loving me through my feelings and I commit to being an extension of that same grace on the earth.

In The Name of Jesus,

Amen

DAY FOUR

PRESS PAUSE: GET YOUR FEELINGS OUT OF THE EQUATION

"When they hurled their insults at him, he did not retaliate; when he suffered, he made no threats. Instead, he entrusted himself to him who judges justly." 1 Peter 2:23 KJV

At times you may feel that your feelings and how you feel is of the utmost importance. It's really easy to get wrapped into what you're feeling or not feeling and it becomes your guide through the day. Don't let that be the case.

When you begin to understand that you are so much more than just your feelings, this will help change how you handle and deal with matters in your everyday life. It will revolutionize your rationalization when making decisions, understanding people, and being able to let things go. It'll become easier to let things go and not hold onto them as our own personal treasure box.

In life you will experience things that are unfortunate, hurtful, and that may just well be truly unjust. Learning how to deal with those feelings when they arise is key. Knowing that you don't always have to accept every frustration that is sent your way gives you power to maneuver through challenges and cast down those negative things that come to distract you in life.

▶**Press Play:** Picture this for a moment. Imagine rocks, lots of rocks and they are coming at YOU. Some of them are big as a grapefruit, some as small as a pebble, and then some aren't even rocks, they're boulders. They're coming at you from every direction and they are coming fast and at a constant pace. Now put one of your hands up to block the rocks and now the other hand. Quick, duck! Here comes another boulder, you dodged it.

Wow, isn't this tiring? It is tiring and stressful dodging a never-ending avalanche of rocks, day in and day out. But, that's what happens when your heart, mind and soul are not focused on God.

This is what we find ourselves doing a lot of times, we're either letting things come at us and beat us up or we're trying to fight off all the rocks and challenges that come at us, to the point we end up tiring ourselves out. Just because the rocks are coming at you doesn't mean you have to get hit by them. Nobody likes getting hurt everyday! So that's why we put our hands so we don't have to be struck by every thing that comes our way.

When problems and situations come at us, big or small, we don't have to let everything affect us all the time. We have to get to a point spiritually where we decide we don't have to get hit by everything thrown and we'll begin to find, by Pressing Pause with God, that He gives good instructions and answers our requests for help. We begin to see that He and His angels have been willing and ready to fight along with us the whole time. God is right there ready to help us walk in victory! Remember, Jesus won the war at Calvary!

Here's the strategy.

If you can just allow yourself to set your mind on God first thing in the morning and then consistently throughout your day, as the boulders come you'll be equipped to handle it. The more you trust God with those boulders, the greater the grace you have to walk in reveals itself. Before you know it, your hands won't even have to go up, because you trust him as a spiritual force field that will be there as it has always been.

Today I challenge you not to stress about life's rocks and boulders, but to accept that you are more than your feelings. You are more than what you see in front of you. Give your feelings to God and allow him to fill you with feelings that are true and that come from a whole and healthy heart.

(| |) Press Pause: One of the best takeaways in regards to your feelings is to guard them. So many times people allow themselves to be the dumping ground for others. You may take on situations and problems that are not yours to take on. You may allow yourself to over think things and before you know it you're "feeling some type of way," because you did not embrace the PRESS PAUSE way of filtering the situation.

One of the greatest things you can do is to develop the art being a ***"Feelings Sorter."*** This simply means, when someone tries to dump their feelings or their emotions on you, you sort through it.

You ask:

Is this really how they feel?

Is this my problem or situation to take on?

Am I assigning someone else's responsibility to me instead of them?

Is this situation really about me?

If you can learn to do this, you can propel your life towards spiritual and natural maturity so rapidly that it will absolutely amaze you.

Sometimes our feelings have other things attached to them. This doesn't make it 100% right and doesn't make it 100% wrong, but how you respond determines the outcome. Choose to look at every encounter in life with God's eyes and be able to gracefully navigate through life with peace and joy. When you abandon the old way of filtering your challenges, you'll grow spiritually and mature in character.

Before you start your day, take a moment to PRESS PAUSE and ask yourself some questions while reflecting on what you read today. Record your responses and hold yourself accountable to walking these responses out on your journey.

Do you find yourself focusing more on the rocks and boulders that are coming at you than on God?

____

____

____

What are two things that you can implement today that will help you focus on God and not on the things around you?

STRATEGY ONE

____

____

____

STRATEGY TWO

Brainstorm at least two boundaries that you can set in your life that will help when dealing with difficult people or situations in the future.

BOUNDARY ONE

BOUNDARY TWO

Thoughts & Reflections:

Fast-forward: Father I know that I have not always been willing to get out of my own way and allow you to work in different areas of my life, but today I surrender. I give you permission to heal my heart and help me to deal with my feelings. Help me to no longer wear my feelings on my shoulder and help me to no longer hold my feelings in. Lord today I give you that treasure box that I have built up and put my feelings in. Today I empty it out before you. As I pour them out to you, I receive your healing and restoration. Fill me with the joy, strength, and determination I need to step outside of myself and into you. Today I step into a new way of dealing with life when it comes to my feelings. Thank you for this season of growth and maturity.

In the name of Jesus,

Amen.

DAY FIVE

PRESS PAUSE: YOUR ATTITUDE

"You are the salt of the earth... you are the light of the world..." Matt 5:13-14 KJV

It's day five and it's time to address the "Big A," better known as your attitude. Take a minute and think about your attitude, can we sum it up in two or three words? What three words describe your attitude? Would it be happy, easy-going, and positive? Would it be always right or we can get along as long as you don't cross me? Or... would you fall right in between I have my good days and I have my bad days?

No matter where you fall, you have to continually make sure that you have a check and balance system set up to evaluate your attitude at all times. Oftentimes, people think that even if they are usually happy and positive that this is not necessary, but EVERYONE needs to keep a pulse on their temperament in order to live a balanced and peaceful life.

►**Press play:** When you look at someone who is happy, easy-going, and positive it seems like everything is all good in their life, right? Now while things may be good for the most part, this attitude type can find themselves being so accustomed to being happy that even when they are not happy, they will portray themselves as happy. It's not something that is done intentionally, however, the habit of happiness can at times desensitize you to the moments when you're not operating with a good attitude. Even the happiest of people have moments of frustration or perceiving things the wrong way.

If I know that overall I'm a happier person, I don't tend to focus on negative things, but if I'm off-balance and maybe you say something to me the wrong way or you try to help me with my attitude I may immediately become defensive because in my mind I know I don't have a problem in that area. This is why even the happiest of the happiest need checks and balances.

For the easy-going checks and balances are important for a different reason. Like the happy temperament, you may be so used to going with the flow that you go with the flow even when it's not profitable for you. You might let too many things go or slide. You may not be apt to quickly address issues and before you know it, you are faced with frustrations and commitments that you never intended to deal with. Before you know it, your life is consumed with other people's priority and that it not the life that you were created to live.

You've looked at the happy temperament and explored the easy going, next take a look at the positive temperament. Just like the other temperaments, being positive is not a bad thing. On the contrary, I believe that it is an excellent thing that everyone should choose to walk in, however, even positivity needs checks and balances.

There are times when positive people need checks and balances, which I'll call from here out CB. The positive temperament's CB is making sure that you are coming across to people around you as positive, but approachable. Just because you may have a more positive attitude, people that aren't used to that don't necessarily understand how you can continually be positive in almost every situation. That misperception can be interpreted as not being genuine and can be perceived as being prideful or unapproachable. Positive people often hear feedback from others such as, "I can't really talk to you, because you'll never understand. Nothing ever goes wrong in your life, you are so perfect."

As someone with a positive temperament, never change your position of positivity, but do be aware of how you engage others with your stance. Use your positive power to unlock a place of peace in the lives that you interact with. Be aware of when your conviction of positivity is hindering someone from tapping into his or hers. Do not boast in your positivity but instead empower others to see things from a brighter perspective.

Now that you have focused on the positive temperaments, there other attitude areas where CB becomes more obvious. This is when you have an attitude that says, "We'll be great as long as you don't rub me the wrong way." This can set you up for problems in different areas of your life. It's easy to be nice to people when they are nice to you.

You are much better than that! No, you don't

deserve someone else's bad day, but you don't have to mirror that moment back to them. You should never be dependent on the actions or reactions of someone else's attitude. Just because someone comes to you with a negative, disrespectful, or nasty attitude does not mean that you should jeopardize your character for him or her. Make a choice to say, "Regardless of how someone is acting I'm going to stay true to my character to the best of my abilities." In doing this you leave the ball in their court. *They always say, "It takes two to tango,"* and very few people will continue to tango over long periods of time by themselves.

You can avoid a lot of unnecessary stress by choosing to press pause and reflect on what's going on, call on the Lord to help you to answer the right way and respond properly. When you're done, you don't even think about it anymore, you waste no extra time or effort on it.

Finally, for the "I have my good days and I have my bad days," CB is equally important. I know in life you have days that are on the top of the mountain and then there are days you're in a valley. With that, you want to make sure that just because a day might seem like there's a lot going on or you really don't feel like being nice, you don't just surrender to your feelings. Sometimes you can see things starting to go in an unproductive direction, but you own the power to take back your day. This is where you choose to balance your attitude. Just because at the start of the day you were low doesn't mean that the rest of your day is doomed.

(| |) Press Pause: You have to learn how to pick yourself up with God, focus on his words and ways, ask him to help you adjust your attitude, and move you forward with a great attitude. It's not always about what's come up in the day that can get you off balance, sometimes it is about allowing what has happened to have more of a ripple effect then it ever should have had. You should look at it like being a little pebble the hits the windshield of your car, when the pebble hits the windshield hard enough it may have a small little mark, but if we allow ourselves to fall into the attitude trap we may look up and it goes from a pen size hole to a crack running the entire length of the windshield.

Don't live your life by allowing little pebbles to have a long-term ripple effect on your day. Don't live your life allowing other people to be able to change the course of your day or your spiritual environment. Remember, you have the power to control your day. Choose joy, choose peace, and choose contentment, even in the face of opposition, crisis, frustration or trial. You can only control what you can control and that is YOU!

When you stand in that truth and press pause on your attitude, you become an extension of God's grace and love on earth. As Christians, wherever you fall within these categories you must remember that ultimately you are the salt and light of the world. You have to pay special attention to your own attitudes and how you conduct yourself from day to day. Choose to be an ambassador of joy! Take time today to be more aware of how others perceive your attitude and what kind of attitude you're giving off.

What attitude category do you sit in the most?

____

Do you find your attitude being more positive or negative?

____

____

____

____

Is your attitude a good representation of God?

____

____

____

____

____

____

What are two practical checks and balances that you will implement for your attitude and how it comes off to others?

1. ______________________________

____

____

____

____

____

____

2. ______________________________

____

____

____

____

____

____

⇨**Fast Forward**: Father God, I pray today that as I go through this life-changing journey of self-reflection with you that you would refine my character and help me to show up in life with an attitude that reflects the beauty of your Word. Show me how to walk balanced and upright as an ambassador of your character in my everyday actions. I thank you that I walk in a faith-filled demeanor that radiates the love of Christ at all times.

In the name of Jesus,

Amen.

DAY SIX

PRESS PAUSE: PREDISPOSITIONS

"The people of Jerusalem and their rulers did not recognize Jesus, yet in condemning him they fulfilled the words of the prophets that are read every Sabbath." Acts 13:27 KJV

Predisposition

The tendency to a condition or quality, usually based on combined efforts of genetic and environmental factors. (i.e. A predisposition to think optimistically or a predisposition to look at things negatively)

▶**Press Play**: No matter who you are or what stage in life you are in, you have experienced or are still experiencing predispositions because of the way you were brought up, your environment, your family, the things you were taught at school, and even the churches you were brought up in. Although different things, all people are exposed to life experiences that shape your actions, character, and values.

Where many get stuck is surrendering to these predispositions without further investigation as to whether they are healthy, productive or fruitful in their life. Don't be that person. Just because you were exposed to a certain way of going about things, does not mean that it is beneficial to continue in that course of action. Oftentimes you won't even recognize these habits until you have a press pause experience with God to uncover these areas.

Predisposition can be very tricky. These are things that you could have had since you were twelve years old, things that we were exposed to, the habits of your family or your parents. Maybe you grew up in church a certain way or you didn't grow up in church. These things can play a factor. If you grew up in church it may be easy for you to look at things spiritually, see behind the actual situation, and discern that there is something spiritual going on. In like manner, if you haven't grown up in church and it may be hard for you to understand people that have and how they discern things or may see things in the spiritual realm.

The same can be said for geographical dispositions. Maybe you grew up in a certain area or culture. It may have impacted you more than another, a lot of times it's hard for us to understand other people and it's only because we may have different backgrounds.

(III) Press Pause: It is important for you to press pause daily in the morning so you can be more in tune with God's heart for the things you were predisposed to in the past that you need to look at. You don't want to continue to operate in those ways or have those certain prejudgments, thoughts, action or the lack of action, because you feel a certain way about things, places and/or people. Press Pause throughout your day so when things are brought to you through situations or circumstances you may face, you take that pause that is well needed before you move forward respond, re-act, or even think.

It is important that you see God before you see situations through your predispositions. Whether simple or serious, it is important to identify the root of your actions. A predisposition can cloud your judgment and have you making decisions that aren't beneficial for your life.

For example, some people are predisposed to

seeing the glass half empty instead of half full because of their upbringing. When life brings them a difficult situation, they immediately think the worse, because they are predisposed to think that it is bad. It's the same for those who have experienced reoccurring disappointment. When you have always had negative experiences, you expect negative things to happen. Learning to press pause when situations present themselves in your life will help you identify predispositions that will keep you from experiencing a full and abundant life.

With the predispositions it can be simple things or it can be serious things. It may be as simple as I don't understand this person because they did or didn't grow up in church or it may be as serious as I don't understand why there are certain things that are always happening to me.

As a believer, the power of life and death is in your tongue. If you always think negative, you expect negative, you are actually drawing negative things closer to you. Your belief system drives your actions. When you harbor negativity in your heart you will begin to expect it in your mind to happen. Those thoughts lead to confessions and your words direct your actions down an unproductive path. That is why you have to be very cautious of what you're speaking.

Just because you have experienced tough times in life, doesn't mean your whole life has to be negative. Sometimes you have to evaluate the negative things that you have experienced, look at the results, and allow God to reveal what is behind those experiences. That's why it is so important to understand your predispositions in order to tackle life's issues.

Allow God to remove some of the roots that may be hindering you from moving forward in life and having a great life with God. You are well able to shatter every predisposition and have a powerful life with the Lord.

1. Identify at least two predispositions that you allowed to get in the way of your judgment at times.

1) ______________________________

____

____

____

2)______________________________

____

____

____

2. What are some ways that you can remove your dispositions and in place devise a straightforward way of thinking?

____

____

____

____

____

3. In what ways do you think by having more of a straightforward way of thinking will enhance your life?

Thoughts & Reflections:

⇨**Fast Forward**: Father, help me to be aware of the things that I need to change that have been deeply rooted over the years. Give me an understanding and wisdom to have your mind, not just to do what I've always done, but do want you want me to do.

In the Jesus name,

Amen.

DAY SEVEN

PRESS PAUSE:" YOUR HABITS

"Set your minds on things above, not on earthly things." Colossians 3:2 KJV

Look at here... it's your good old habits... well, well, well. A habit is a learned or developed behavior pattern regularly followed until it has become almost involuntary. You may have always done something, but somewhere down the line you've learned and developed your habit. Just because it may feel like you've always done something, does not mean that it has to stay apart of your life. It is said, "It takes twenty-one days to break a habit." That may vary for different people, but keep that in mind.

It is a lot easier to make a habit than it is to break one. One of my goals with this thirty-day journey to a new lifestyle is to challenge you BEYOND that twenty-one day timeframe to help you break barriers and create new productive habits. Some of the habits you may have feel normal now, but they're not and you are about to break them and then step into a brand new normal.

▶**Press Play**: I had a habit of being late for years. I was so late to things that people knew to either give me a different time or just expect me to be there twenty minutes late. Like most with a bad habit, I eventually became very aware of my tardy habit and although I no longer WANTED to be late, I was still not showing up on time. For years, I began to actively work on my timeliness. This particular year, it was beginning to affect everything around me including my business, my family, and even my reputation at the church. I began to be labeled as a late person and although it was my truth, I hated it. What habits have labeled you?

Even though I was always late to things after a while I never wanted to be late and found myself frustrated when I began to notice it happening. I will never forget this turning point in my life. Things were going great in my life then slowly during this one season I noticed things beginning to slow down. I had been praying and seeking the Lord trying to figure out what was going on and the Lord gave me a prophetic word.

This is in a time that I had prophetic words coming of the great things that God had planned for my life. When I got up there and my pastor begin to speak, he simply told me obedience is better than sacrifice and God was basically holding off on some blessings for my life because even though I sacrificed, worked in the church on Sundays or whenever I was needed, I was not walking in obedience. Those prayers I had been praying for and seeking God for the answers were there, but he was not going to release them until I started to walk in obedience.

Sometimes the things we want and pray for have already been answered and if I had pressed pause with God asking him about the things I have or need to work on he would've already show me, but instead I had to be shown in a way that got my attention. I knew it was on point as God had already confirmed that exact word that morning to me about my timeliness.

(| |) Press Pause: Everyone has habits right? Being late was mine and I was known for it. We joked about it and people understood it, but when it came to God, that area was still disobedience. In the church God may want to use us in a much greater way but how can he gives us things or use us if we're not or have not positioned ourselves in a place to be used in a greater way. Being late and not coming in on time was not a good look even within the church.

God wants obedience in every area and because we may have become accustomed to, gotten content with or want to overlook an area does not make it any less important to God. For me my habit was time and God had started to show me how it can affect me in the different areas of my life. I didn't want to be known for those things, but I didn't see progress until I stopped making excuses and focused on God. I had to focus on God and know that I can do this through Christ; I had to look at God and say, "God give me the strategy I need to be able to walk in this obedience. I don't want my relationship with people around me and even more importantly my relationship with God, to be strained because of disobedience." Once I began to become obedient to God, I began to see the blessings that God had already surrounded my life with start to flow again in a stronger way. God was still blessing me at that time, but it was not at the level I had known him to do in the past. I was stuck in a level and God had something greater for me, but I had this invisible block that I couldn't break through, which was disobedience.

Once I got in line with my obedience, it broke the boundary that I had put in place and God was able to take me to another level in him. Now I don't have the testimony of having a habit of smoking, being delivered from drinking, pornography, or different things others may have, but it's time for you to deal with whatever habits you have.

Allow God to break those things so you can walk through the path that he has set before you. If you attempt to go around, under, or over your bad habits you may not respect that it's something serious. No matter how seemingly simple or serious the habit is, no matter what area or what level you may think you're at, if it's disobedience, a hindrance or a road block, it is that important to remove it to move forward in life. If it was important enough for God to shine the light in the area that he shined it in, it's important enough to overcome.

Refuse to tie God's hands by not dealing with bad habits and walking in disobedience to his word. Sometimes you pray for things and are waiting for things to happen, but because of your disobedience and not following his instructions God cannot move. The blessing, the gift, or the answer is there, but he may not be able to fully move because you've gone against his word and he is not a man that he should lie. If he tells you that this is the way to do it, that's what he means. You cannot try to go around things, overlook things, dismiss things and still expect for him to work and move.

You don't want to ignore the things that come to the light because God has shined a light on them for a reason. If those habits and things in your life are hindering you or your relationship with God, deal with them. Don't worry about if it feels to great to you or to simple, it's all the same in God's eyes.

Remember, God brings these habits to the surface because he wants you whole. He can give you compassion remove any guilt or shame from it for you to deal with it and move on from it. Don't be shamed into keeping or holding onto a habit that God as shine light on because you're embarrassed or ashamed. Walk through this with God, you need to hit the pause button, center your eyes on God, and move forward with him. Let' God dig up those things and get them out so you can be healed, whole, and God can fill you with a new good godly habit that you have no need to be ashamed of.

1. Do you have habits that have gotten in the way of you moving forward in a certain area in your life?

2. What things have those habits caused you to miss out on?

3. What are three steps that you can take to remove this habit from your life?

1. ______________________________
2. ______________________________
3. ______________________________

4. List one good Godly habit you can replace your bad habit with.

____
____
____
____
____

Thoughts & Reflections:

____
____
____
____
____
____

⇨**Fast forward**: Father God help me with my habits and give me the strength I need to change and make new Godly habit with you. Please take out any guilt, embarrassment, or feeling of shame that I may want to carry from my mistakes. I know that you are with me and that your comfort and protection is surrounding me as I grow stronger in you.

In the name of Jesus,

Amen.

PRESS PAUSE: RELATIONSHIPS

Relationships are key factors when it comes to important areas of your life. Your relationships with the people around you, to include our family, friends, associates and co-workers, can play a vital role in your decision-making as you get to know yourselves on a different level. These relationships are good and important, but you have to make sure that within every area of these different relationships that they are good, strong, and healthy.

There's no reason to surround yourself with people who are dysfunctional. You need life-giving relationships to help you learn how to get along with others, grow, and understand differences. If you nurture your relationships right, they can be some of the biggest blessings for your life.

DAY EIGHT

PRESS PAUSE: WITH YOUR PARTNER

"Husbands, go all out in your love for your wives, exactly as Christ did for the church—a love marked by giving, not getting. Christ's love makes the church whole. His words evoke her beauty. Everything he does and says is designed to bring the best out of her, dressing her in dazzling white silk, radiant with holiness. And that is how husbands ought to love their wives. They're really doing themselves a favor—since they're already "one" in marriage...

...And this provides a good picture of how each husband is to treat his wife, loving himself in loving her, and how each wife is to honor (respect) her husband."

Ephesians 5:25-33 KJV

How do you deal when faced with a difficult situation when it comes to someone that you love? It's not always easy to take the higher road, but the benefits of doing so will always be worth it.

▶**Press Play:** Thinking on my conversation the other day with a friend, she shared with me about how her son and his wife were not getting along and how his household was in an uproar. They were either not speaking to each other or they were arguing and fighting all the time. It appeared to be no love in the household, only coldness and disconnection.

As my friend and her son began to go deeper in conversation, she was baffled by all of the things she was hearing that was going on in their household. She asked her son to stop for a second, because she wanted to help him identify the root of their problems.

She started by asking him to think back on what happened prior to their present problems and pinpoint what has contributed to the chaos they were currently experiencing. As he reflected back his story went something like this...

He hadn't spoken to his wife for over two weeks, primarily because he felt that all she did was fuss and argue with him about not helping around the house and the time he was spending with friends. He went on to say that he felt that he deserved his time to himself and with his friends because he worked hard. Besides, he cannot be penalized for his wife not having friends. In his mind, she was being selfish and ***THAT*** *was what was causing all of* *their marital problems.*

Stop! Let's press pause for a moment in this scenario. This is a prime example how reflection can be good or bad. If done wrong you spend time hours even days replaying an event or situation over and over again to yourself in your head and not coming to a solution.

This type of reflecting can rob you of your joy, peace, and ability to see matters of the heart clearly, because you're only looking at your situation from one perspective. Press pause moments are not effective if you reflect with a closed mind or a closed heart.

Okay, let's press play again on this situation.

Like any good communicator, my friend lets her son continue for a while, because clearly he needed to release these feelings from his heart. It is important in tough situations to let a person vent before trying to present different perspectives or solutions. This allows them an opportunity to be heard and feel heard. That way when you move forward it can be done without resistance.

Instead of imposing her point of view, she meekly asked him for permission to share with him an outside perspective free from emotion, frustration or bias since she is not personally involved in their situation.

⇦ **Press Rewind:** In relationships, a great way to evaluate a situation is though a series of facts followed by questions. My friend choose this approach with her son.

Fact One: His wife asked on several occasions to help around the house, help with the four children and taking on some household chores.

Fact 2: Both the son and his wife work full-time jobs, however the wife has the additional responsibility to managing the household.

Follow-up Question: Do you think that she could be overwhelmed trying to manage maintaining her career and then coming home to cook, clean, help with homework and keeping the house in order by herself?

Response: The son's initial response was still one-dimensional. His thoughts were, "I always tell her if she would only try to plan out her day she could get this done and wouldn't have to nag me so much about it. I even told her I would help her make a schedule."

Clarify The Response: Now my friend had a few choices to approaching his response. The appropriate response when helping someone press pause or even taking yourself through a press pause moment, is to repeat back the response in the form of a question, this time including the facts.

So my friend looks at her son and says, "So what you are saying is that although you both work full time jobs, you feel that the best way for your wife to not feel overwhelmed with managing the household is not for you to pitch in, but for her to become more organized. And your contribution is to help her become more organized to do it on her own, is this what you are saying?

Now as you are reading this, do you see how ridiculous his perspective sounds once his response is echoed back with the facts? It's the same way for you in your own relationship experiences. When you look at things from your own point of view, you miss the bigger picture and can hinder yourself from finding mutual agreements that bring peace into the home.

Explore The Results: Every action has a reaction. Take a look at the results of seeing it only from your perspective. The next step for my friend was to now echo the results of his reasoning.

She looks at her son and say, "So that I understand you correctly, you're tired of the nagging, fussing and continual arguing so you decided to remove yourself mentally from the situation by stopping communication with her. As a result, you aren't talking to one another. Even more, the kids are able to see the disconnection, they now feel unstable, and are beginning to act out as well and your wife getting herself together is the only logical way for you all to solve the problem. Are these the results that you really want or are you willing to look at this again from a wider perspective?

(| |) Press Pause: It is in this moment that a person can clearly see not only that are they approaching a situation from a one-sided perspective, but that perspective is hindering them from having positive results.

When dealing with relationships its highly

important to remove your emotions and think about the situation from the other person's perspective. Ask yourself how they feel or what they may be experiencing. If my friend's son was to do that, he would see that her heart is in managing the home was not to nag him, but to provide a comfortable and loving environment for him and their family. Her frustration really resides in not being able to provide that on her own. When she is asking for help, she's asking for partnership and when he realizes the place of love this desire comes from, it will be easier to find mutual solutions within the relationship.

It's not that she was right and he was wrong or vice versa, it was about hearing and responding in a manner that yields positive solutions that build and betters the household. Just like in the Press Pause process there is a time and place for your feelings to be heard, you must be open to hearing the heart of your spouse or significant other.

It is vital that you never check out in a time of need, especially for our family. No matter what you are facing, you have to be present to press through, even if you don't know how to solve what you're going through. Press Pause when you are in the middle of or faced with adversity. Go sit down with God, ask him for clarity, and to take out anything that may be obstructing your vision to see things clearly.

In this scenario you can also ask yourself why did he take her actions straight to nagging. Is it just what was asked of him or is it something else that's in his mind that the minute someone asked more than once or twice it's considered nagging? What was unseen was his past relationships and the nagging and arguing that occurred in them.

Until you sit down in your heart with the help of God, how can you know where some of these issues are coming from? Unresolved things in the past that were never addressed or dealt with can come up and manifest in different areas in your present relationships.

When it comes to relationships pressing pause is more than just looking deeper into your response and actions, it's being able to also explore the heart of the other person through God's eyes. Be committed to letting God take you beneath the surface and discover what is keeping you from having an abundant relationship.

Choose not to let the things of the past or small misunderstandings lead you down avoidable roads. This is the perfect time to Press Pause.

1. Have you ever lost focus in your relationship and allowed things to get in the way of you doing the right thing?

____

____

____

____

____

____

____

2. Do you find yourself acting or responding negatively because of the way your partner has acted towards you?

____

____

3. What two strategies will you use in the future to not let small things get in the way of doing the right thing in your relationship?

4. What is something positive you can do when your partner is acting negative towards you that will help strengthen your relationship?

5. Find a scripture on love, write it down, and remember it to help you speak life into your relationship.

Thoughts & Reflections:

⇨**Fast forward**: Dear father please help me to do the right things in my relationship and keep me aware of my press pause moments. Help me to seek you in those moments before I move forward so that I can always keep a loving attitude towards my partner.

In the name of Jesus,

Amen.

DAY NINE

PRESS PAUSE: YOUR RELATIONSHIP WITH YOUR PARTNER

"Nevertheless I have somewhat against thee, because thou hast left thy first love."

Revelation 2:4 KJV

How would you view your relationship? Is it healthy, whole, and fulfilling? Does it bring joy and peace to your life? Would you consider it to be an honorable committed relationship or is there more shame and lack of commitment?

▶**Press Play:** No matter where you fall within your relationship, one of the most important questions would be does this relationship bring honor not only to yourself in being true to who you are, but more importantly does it bring honor and glory to God. Often in life people get caught up in the search, the need, and desire for love that they can occasionally get lost in the dream of love. Now while love can be true and is real, the dream of love can sometimes be more of an illusion in your mind than in your reality.

Most people have this idea in their head of what love looks like for them. You may have that "list" of what love looks like, acts like, and feels like, but in your pursuit for love you end up with only a fragment of what you dreamed of. When you face that reality, you also face the truth that this person may not be able to provide you with the full picture of love you originally set out for.

Sometimes this comes in the form of settling and other times it comes in the form of compromise, but in order to have a healthy and fulfilling life you have to evaluate how a relationship impacts the totality of you as a person. Ask yourself, "Have I settled or have I compromised?"

Let's look at a scenario. You have this list of ten things you need from a partner. You meet Mr. or Ms. Right, but they only have three of the ten attributes. You continue with the relationship, but you find yourself frustrated because you're not getting what you really want or need. When you compromise you won't feel slighted by what you are missing, because what you must understand is that you gave up something to receive something else. When you settle, you simply go lacking in those areas.

The more you try to overlook, adjust, rearrange, or change your partner to make them fit into what you truly desire, the more you're forcing what you truly desire into that dream of love. You will never be satisfied settling. You'll always seek what you are missing and you will remain unfulfilled.

Let's look at another scenario. Your dream of love consists of your being in a committed relationship with a partner who is faithful, understanding, loyal, loving, trustworthy, and God-fearing. You are in a relationship with someone who is still finding out who they want to be. They are not even sure if they want to be in a committed relationship or married.

You've settled for companionship without commitment and in return you tell yourself things like, "We are not ready for marriage. Marriage isn't for everyone. It's just not time for us to focus on marriage." In one massive statement you have completely altered who you are to fit into the idea of love. You have settled and denied yourself the gift of true love. You deserve a love that doesn't require you to compromise who you are. Choose not to settled, but to wait for the one that fits without major adjustments.

(| | |) **Press Pause:** What many often miss in this process is that in their quest for that dream love your attempts to change your partner doesn't just effect them. It directly impacts you. When you try to rearrange and maneuver relationships and people to be what you need or want them to be, you end up changing who you are, what you really want, and how you really feel you should be treated and respected.

Don't try to fit people into your idea of who you think they should be. When you want somebody or your relationship to be a certain way, the areas that you have overlooked will start to show up more pronounced. This then forces you to react and change your viewpoint in order to keep the relationship within the alignment of your true desire.

God has the ability to bring into your life a man or a woman that will add to your quality of life. A partner should add value and bring out positive qualities and gifts that you don't even know exist. When you press pause and trust God to bring you someone you don't have to settle for, you will experience a new kind of love.

Take time to really think about what you want in a partner. Ask God to lead, guide, and give you the strength, will, and determination to stay focused and not to stray away from the things that he has for you when distractions come along.

1. Have you let your want and need for love (real love) outweigh what you really want form a partner?

____

____

____

____

____

____

____

2. Did you get what you really wanted or did you end up settling for somewhere in-between?

3.What are some steps you can take to help yourself wait on God to find the right person that will be all you desire them to be?

4.Do you have a true picture of who you really want and what you're truly looking for?

Thoughts & Reflections:

⇨**Fast forward:** Father God please go before me when choosing the right person you have for me. Help me to wait on you and not be led by my feelings or my personal desires. Give me the tools I need to see you as the head of my relationship and allow you to lead me in the right direction in my life personally and spiritually. Father God I thank you for loving me enough to give me all that I need and the ability to wait on you.

In the name of Jesus,

Amen.

DAY TEN

PRESS PAUSE WITH YOUR FAMILY

"Make a clean break with all cutting, backbiting, profane talk. Be gentle with one another, sensitive. Forgive one another as quickly and thoroughly as God in Christ forgave you." Ephesians 4:32 KJV

There are so many dynamics that encompass our family circumstances and makeup. There are different areas when it comes to our family dynamic. Press Pause With Your Family alone could be it's own devotional, because there are so many different situations that affect the family. Today you will focus on the family as a whole and the areas that you need to press pause in the most.

Family is the one thing that you can't choose, but you must deal with. There can be a lot of emotions and feelings along with hurt and pain in some cases. Family members have wounded many people and it can be tough to push forward, but you have the ability to heal and have life-giving relationships with those you are bonded to by blood and love.

▶**Press Play:** When focusing on the family today, it's best to look at yourself. There could be deep-rooted things that have taken place throughout the years that are affecting your family life. It could be dealing with family members that are stubborn and unwilling to change or a family secret where someone hurt you and never admitted. These are things in your family life that make it extremely difficult to move on. In the face of those situations, what you must understand is that you can only change you. As much as you may want that apology, you may never get it. Be willing to deal with what you can control and that is you!

When family hurt goes unaddressed or unhealed, it's easy to allow that pain to spill over into other areas in your life. Don't be willing to allow someone else's refusal to heal keep you from walking in wholeness. Sometimes you have to be willing to adjust your responses so that family issues don't haunt your life. You deserve that! Focus on the things you can change. Let God deal with your part and allow him to fill the other voids. There are going to be certain circumstances and situations that you will not be able to change or fixed by going to and or addressing a person to get to or find the root of the problem. However, there is one thing you are always able to change, YOU.

The balance to dealing with family issues is learn how to love others without unrealistic expectations. You shouldn't use family issues as a reason to stop talking to or isolating yourself from family. You simply learn to dwell with them according to knowledge. If your aunt is negative, accept that, believe that God will heal the areas in her life that have hardened her heart and learn to guard the things that are precious to you when you interact with her so that her posture does not interrupt yours.

You do not have to own other people's "crazy" or issues or pain! When we learn to press pause on the difficult behavior a family member is pushing out, you will often find that it really isn't about you. That family member is nine times out of ten dealing with some underlying issues that had affected their behavior. Don't take it personal, be the light in their darkness by not dishing back to them what they dish out.

It's time to look at your family from a different perspective. Instead of seeing what they have done to you, choose to allow God to show you how you can positively impact them. You possess the ability to show your family Christ when you react in a God-centered manner. Today I challenge you to dig deep and ask yourself, "How can I show my family God?" Look at this in every family dynamic in your life. Do you need to be more patient? Do you need to come around more often? Do you need to forgive?

You are the link to peace in your family and when you press pause during difficult family problems, you create room for God to help you develop a healthy family.

(| |) Press Pause: Today you are digging deep with an extended amount of questions to really explore your family dynamic. No matter what you have experienced with a family member, this is your moment to move forward. Sometimes you can allow things that are closer to you hinder you. It does not have to be that way at all. Expect God to give you a strategy to love them without being hurt by them. He's able!

What are two things that stop you from interacting with your family?

____

____

____

____

____

What has caused relationships to be difficult in your family?

____

____

____

____

____

____

How can you change how you deal with and interact with your family?

____

____

____

____

Write out your vision of a happy and healthy family life.

____

____

____

What three steps can you take to make that vision come true?

____

____

____

List two scriptures that will help support your healthy family vision.

Scripture 1:

____

____

____

Scripture 2:

____

____

____

Thoughts & Reflections:

⇨ **Fast forward:** Father God I bring my family before for you, asking you to touch the hearts of us all. Everything that has been done or not done, I place in your hands. As I give it all to you, I ask you to clean my heart from any hurt and old wounds. Make me whole in you. Shower me with your love and comfort, knowing that you are my father, my love, and my friend. Touch my heart and my mind to not want to take any burden back on myself. I thank you for your love and kindness.

In Jesus name,

Amen.

DAY ELEVEN

PRESS PAUSE WITH CLOSE FRIENDS

"The righteous choose their friends carefully, but the way of the wicked leads them astray."
Proverbs 12:26

Friendships are a very important part of our lives, we don't want to go through life not having or wanting friends. The right friends can be a blessing sent from heaven and being linked up with the wrong friends can feel like a curse from hell. We should always have friends; they are our circles of support physically, mentally, emotionally and spiritually. The right friends add value and enrichment to our lives.

Friends may change depending on what situation or season we're in, but in all they help us grow and learn how to deal with and understand differences in people. Friendships give us the ability to embrace differences and learn to live and grow together. It is important that we have and make healthy long-lasting friendships. It is also as essential that we have the right friends in our lives. Think of it this way, "Its better to have three trustworthy, loyal, and honest friends than twenty fake, un-trustworthy, and un-loyal friends.

We must get with God on the people that we choose to keep company with. Although it is important that we learn how to deal with and get along with people, we can't just choose anyone to befriend. There is a significant difference between loving people and being an extension of God's love to people and bringing them into our inner circle. Choose your circle of friends prayerfully. There's no wrong or right number of friends, however, you do want to make sure that those intimate relationships are life-giving.

While having friends is helpful for our growth spiritually as well as naturally, there are a few common misconceptions about friends and friendships. These misconceptions are commonly overlooked and when initiated out of balance, can create problems and stunt your growth.

The first common misconception is that it's okay to only have friends of the opposite gender. We hear it all the time, women who boldly declare, "I don't have female friends, because females are __________. I only hang out with males." Or men who say, "My friends are all female. I don't have male friends." The fact that this misconception starts with only is the first red flag that this is an unhealthy perception of people and friendships.

While it is okay to have healthy friendships with people of the opposite gender, it is not healthy or balanced when you ONLY choose to befriend one gender. This train of thought is usually rooted in some form of hurt from the past. Some people feel that it's hard for them to make friends in their same gender. Others have had bad experiences with a gender so they have lumped everyone in the same category.

Both genders have something valuable that they add to a person's life. Someone of the same gender will understand things about you that the other won't. Men need those bonding moments with men. Women need bonding moments with women. When we disregard the value in those relationships we go lacking in our lives.

If you cannot get along with anyone that's in your gender, if you're male and you can't get along with any males or if you're female and you can't get along with any female, you need to press pause and find the root of those feelings. Contrary to popular opinion, it's not always that someone is jealous of you. Everyone is not "hating" on you. Sometimes that can be a factor, but you would have to evaluate those friendships on a case-by-case basis.

Now that we have established that everyone is not the problem, ask yourself, "Have I looked at the type of people that I've been seeking friendship from?" Have I looked at my own motives?"

It's critical to check your motives. If you're looking at people for what you can do for them or what they can do for you, you are going to be more prone to choose unhealthy friendships. So let's not continue to do the same things and expect a different result. Step outside your comfort zone and look at people that can complement you, that are somewhere that you may want to get to, and check your motives before seeking friends next time.

It's good to challenge ourselves by finding people that complement us, that are where we want to be in life and have different outlooks on something. Sometimes we need that challenge to come in our lives to help balance us out. Now that doesn't mean that we look for people for what they have and what they don't have, we look in the realm of what could we build and learn from each other.

The second misconception is unhealthy friendships don't have a big impact on us. Often we think, "I can handle them and keep their dysfunction to a minimum in my life." Thinking we can handle or keep certain friendships at a distance and they not have a real effect on our lives is unrealistic. At times you have friends that pull on you for different things, they may pull on your time, pull on your attention, or simply pull you away from your dreams and ambitions.

At times you find these friends asking for help, which is not bad, as we all need help from time to time, but they're never willing to help themselves. They may be encouraging you to continue in sin or a destructive path. Maybe they're always dumping, gossiping or having drama surrounding them, they can be your yes man never willing to really tell you the truth especially when you're wrong. Those are the friendships that we need to be prayerful about. Press Pause and let God show you these friendships.

This is also the time that you'll be able to make sure that if you have been that person for others the light will help you in the part of your character that needs to be rooted out. it's easy to say how you don't need friends or we'll walk away from friends without a problem, its harder to say that when God shines a light on someone that we really have grown close to throughout your friendship. Sometimes its the close ones that we know aren't good friendships for us and don't benefit us that God brings to light but we tend to want to hold onto.

▶**Press Play**: I found myself in a situation some year's back where I had a couple of friends that I felt always were pulling and draining my time and my energy. They would want to talk and hang for hours, constantly pulling for my time and attention. I would find myself wanting to relax and do something different. I started to notice that they did not have any real drive or sense of direction for their life. They were always too available and willing to sit around and do nothing all the time.

Although I had things to do and had lots of

ambitions and dreams, I found that the more I would be around them, the more I became stagnant. I begin to see myself making excuses to take breaks and relax more and more. Before long I began to see my dreams, ambitions and goals beginning to move further and further away. I started letting my friendship distract me and before I knew it, I was complacent.

When God starting showing me this and asked me to let go of the friendship, it was very hard. We had years of friendship invested in each other. I was very comfortable with them; I became too comfortable in that friendship. When a friendship stifles your personal growth, it's time to let go and shift that friend into a new position in your life. You cannot move forward with your dreams and ambitions with these types of friendships in you life.

Through all the different stages and seasons in my life, when I allowed God to shine the light in my friendships and I began to trust him with my friends, I began to see things get back on track. I was able to still be friends with some of them, but at a distance. I prayed for them, I still had a love for them, but I didn't have to involve myself with them so closely on a daily basis.

I've also learned that when I didn't remove myself from some friends, God had a way of removing them from my life. Whether it would be a small falling out over something insignificant or something major, I knew what God wanted me to do and I knew exactly where the friction was coming from. Since pressing pause in my friendships, God has always placed new people in my life and I have been able to gain and maintain some amazing life-giving friendships.

Be wise in how you choose your friends; seek God first and foremost for his guidance because friends can play a big role in you reaching your destiny and your full potential.

Who are you friends with?

Who do you hold close in your life?

Who have you allowed into your heart into your mind into your circle of trust?

Have they earned that position?

____

____

____

Have you sought God's insight on those friendships?

____

____

____

____

____

____

(| |) Press Pause: Don't be a dumping ground, letting anyone and anybody get close to your heart. Always seek God first. Give yourself time today and pray with God concerning the people that you have allowed to get close to you. Have your ears open to listen to the people that he points out that you may have allowed to get too close to your heart that should not be. It's okay for us to have close friends and really care about people, but we don't want to have someone close to us that's not good or healthy for us. We also don't want to put anyone closer than what we put God. Make sure that he has our heart and a special place in it. We want to make sure that we honor ourselves in choosing the people that we allow closest to us. Don't let anyone pull you away from your dreams and your destiny in God.

Thoughts & Reflections:

⇨ **Fast forward:** Father I think you that you have allowed us the opportunity to have friends and make good friendships. I pray that you would go before me when it concerns the people I've allowed to be closest to my heart. Show me anyone or anything that I've allowed close to me that is not right for me. Father I believe that having friends are a good thing and they are important in my life. I ask you to help me make the right decisions when choosing my friends. Please help me to know what to look for, what values morals and character that I need in a friend and that a friend needs in me. I love you and I thank you for all that you've done and all that you're doing in my friendship.

In the name of Jesus,

Amen.

DAY TWELVE

PRESS PAUSE IN YOUR RELATIONSHIP WITH YOUR CHURCH FAMILY

"He said to his disciples, "The harvest is great, but the workers are few."

Matthew 9:37

How is your relationship with other believers in Christ? What things would the people that you fellowship with weekly say about you? Will they say that you are kindhearted? Will they say that you're a bold believer? Will they say that you are known to gossip? Will they say that you are easily offended? That you carry a chip on your shoulder? That you keep to yourself? That you are outspoken? Will they say that you only come once in a while? Will they even realize that you have a relationship with God?

The people that you associate with at church should be able to see your walk with Christ. It is important that we show our love for Christ not just to him, but to our brothers and sisters in Christ as well. We need to be very aware of our actions and reactions to the people we fellowship with on a weekly basis at church. It's important as believers in Christ that we help to hold up our fellow believers and befriend them get to know and fellowship with them. Not only inside of church but on the outside of the church walls as well.

Establish good relationships with fellow believers. Be there to hold each other up in times of need and be a great supporter in times of success. We want the body of Christ to be whole so we can stand united when reaching out and giving a helping hand to the lost people in our cities and communities. We want to make sure that we're getting out any gossip, backbiting and hang-ups that may be in us. We want to make sure that we're not being easily offended, bitter, or a downer when it comes to the things of the church.

▶**Press play:** When it comes to the things of God and his church as the body of Christ, he wants and needs us to be healthy and whole-mind, body and spirit. We don't want to continue church as usual where we're constantly helping each other speaking to and uplifting each other. Or we're constantly needing encouragement, needing someone to give a helping hand, needing someone to constantly meet our emotional needs or needing someone to hold our hand continually. It's okay to need help and encouragement at times through our Christian walk and there are times that we all need it. It's okay to uplift each other spiritually as well, because this walk is not always easy. It's not that those things are not good or right to do, they are necessary, but there does come a time in our lives that we need to pull on the strength of God and allow him to spiritually feed us so that we mature and have a strong spiritual strength and faith in him.

(| |) **Press pause:** As we work on ourselves individually and how we treat and interact with our fellow sisters and brothers in Christ, we want to be conscious of our interactions both inside and outside of our church. Let's take time out to make sure that we are growing spiritually, that we are coming off friendly and that we are found trustworthy. The better, stronger, and healthier we are as the body of Christ, the more united and powerful we'll be in our communities and neighborhoods to impact the unsaved.

It is essential that we make every effort to establish great relationships with each other and important for us to be healthy and whole so that we can go out strong and united together to get the harvest that is ready. People are ready for a change. People are looking for guidance, but we must make sure that we as the church are of good character and that we get along with each other.

It's hard to draw the harvest in if we can't get along. They'll see that and let's be real, "who wants to be a part of or around confusion?" If we can't help ourselves or be a support to each other, how can we then go out and try to bring in people that need help as well? Let's take this time to look over our actions, and ourselves.

It's time to really allow God to show us areas that we may not be as strong as we need to be. Let's be conscious and intentional in our relationships. Let's make sure that we look for the best and expect the best with each other in the body of Christ.

Let's not prejudge, overlook, or dismiss anyone but let's look at everyone the same way that Christ does so that we can move forward and have healthy, strong, and whole relationships with each other.

Have you ever misjudged someone in the church only to find that they were nothing like you thought them to be?

____

____

____

____

____

Name at least two areas that you find yourself needing help in as it relates to your church family.

____

____

____

____

____

What are two steps can you take to intentionally make a change and move in a new direction?

____

____

____

____

____

How will being more intentional in these areas effect how you operate in your church?

____

____

____

____

____

What a two things you can do to help your church bring in the harvest?

____

____

____

____

____

Thoughts & Reflections:

⇨**Fast-forward:** Father I think you for giving us places to worship and brothers and sisters to walk alongside us in our Christian walk. I asked that you would help give strength to the areas that I need to become spiritually healthy and mature as a contributing member of the body of Christ. I ask that you would help me to get along with my sisters and brothers and that you would give us the maturity and strength to go out and bring in the harvest. Thank you for giving us these friendships and allowing us to be a part of your body. Please help us to represent you well, as we are a reflection of you.

In the name of Jesus,

Amen.

DAY THIRTEEN

Press Pause On Your Relationship With Your Co-Workers

"Do to others whatever you would like them to do to you. This is the essence of all that is taught in the law and the prophets."

Matthew 7:12 KJV

Things aren't always what they seem and every relationship is important and sometimes can be a reflection of our inner thoughts and feelings.

▶**Press Play:** A friend of mine that works in large corporation is at work; we'll call her Cheryl. Like usual, as the day goes by she gets up walks around her cubicle area to finish her job on the phone. She's talking to clients, discussing and finding solutions for them, and getting all the information that she needs like every other day. She gets a instant message as she is going about her day, glances at it, and notices that its from a fellow coworker in her office. The email simply says,

“Hi Cheryl – I ask that you would not pace the floor next to my cubicle when working.

Thanks a lot,

Lee Ann”

A few minutes go by and Cheryl sits and thinks about the message. She didn’t know why Lee Ann hadn't come to address her face-to-face since they sit a cubicle or two from each other. Cheryl presses pause to reflect back at her actions. She knows that she's not talking loud on the phone and that she is not directly next to Lee Ann walking, but she is next to her cubicle area.

Cheryl doesn’t get it. What could be such a big problem? In search of answers, Cheryl decides to e-mail her boss to get some insight on how to handle the situation. Meanwhile, Lee Ann has passed by Cheryl at least two times without saying anything.

Cheryl’s boss goes on to explain that Lee Ann’s lack of communication is due to a little problem that she’s been having communicating with people in the workplace. He explains that she is uncomfortable with articulating her words and being around people. While Cheryl understands that people are all different, she felt it was more of an underlying issue, which was less about the actual event, but more about her.

This wasn't the first time that Lee Ann was bothered by Cheryl. For some unknown reason Cheryl always seemed to rub Lee Ann the wrong way. What we didn't know was that Lee Ann had a prejudice to Cheryl due to some past predispositions with people of the same ethnicity. Although Cheryl's outer appearance looked like the people she prejudged, she couldn't understand why her actions were so different from what she had in her mind of what they should be like. She wasn't the stereotype that Lee Ann had in her head and that made her uncomfortable.

Now what Lee Ann didn't know, was that Cheryl had a very similar lifestyle. Cheryl was actually raised by multicultural parents that had children with very diverse backgrounds. She never took the time to know that Cheryl didn't have racial boundaries set in place to block her view, because of how she was raised. Cheryl was someone that was very easy to get along with and comfortable in her own skin. Cheryl and LeAnn would've actually got along great and it could have helped LeAnn to understand diversity in the workplace and embrace it a little more.

What can we learn from LeAnn is that it's not always the person we have a problem with, many times it's our own personal predetermined judgment. If LeAnn would've taken a second to press pause, she would have realized that Cheryl's behavior was no different then the others in the office.

(| |)Press Pause: We want to be accountable for our actions no matter where we are or who it's towards. Even on our jobs with our coworkers, we want to make sure that we extend our best foot forward. This was a simple example of something that happened that was not a big ordeal, but it was still a teachable moment. In life and particularly our work life, we will come against and run into people that for whatever reason may not accept us. How do we get along with them? Are they willing to change? Will they see things in a different light or adjust their perceptions? Maybe or maybe not, that's not for us to decide. We are only accountable for our own actions. We want to show the love of Christ no matter where were at, no matter who's watching, and no matter if we think someone deserves it or not. We are learning how to press pause and reflect on who we are. We're strengthening our character and that's what we want to keep our focus on.

Do you have a person that you find it extremely difficult to get along with on your job?

____

____

____

____

What are two things you can do differently that will help you in dealing with that person and help you show the love of Christ to that person?

____

____

____

____

As you learn how to press pause, name one benefit from living this lifestyle that will help you daily at work.

____

____

____

____

____

____

⇨ **Fast-forward**: Father thank you for allowing me to have the opportunity to go to work every day. I ask that you would give me the strength to press pause on my job no matter how difficult the situation. Help me to love the sometimes seemingly unlovable and to be a great representation of you. Help me get along with my coworkers, bosses, and supervisors. Let them see and me see a change.

In Jesus' name,

Amen.

DAY FOURTEEN

PRESS PAUSE: YOUR RELATIONSHIP WITH OTHERS, ACQUAINTANCES, PEERS AND FAMILIAR PEOPLE

The second is equally important: 'Love your neighbor as yourself. No other commandment is greater than these." Mark 12:31

How do the people you see on a daily, weekly, and monthly basis perceive you? What is your relationship like around people that you may see regularly that are not necessarily your friends or in your close circle, but you still have an acquaintance with? Do they know your beliefs? Can they see your walk? What would they say about your character? Would they view you to be someone of good character that's morally sound or would they be shocked to know that you were a Christian?

This is a great place to press pause, because these are not necessarily people that we feel the need to strengthen our relationship with. They're not our friends, family, church family, or significant other, but they are the people that we pass throughout our day from time to time. How we treat these people is more of an indicator of our true character. It can give us more clues into our actions and ways, because many times we often show up as are truest self. We often respect and honor our friendships and inner circle to the point that we watch the way we act and speak. We're consciously and subconsciously more aware of our mannerisms, thoughts, and responses because we don't want to hurt, offended, or be perceived in a certain manner.

These "other people: that we interact with on a daily basis often have a chance to see us with our guards down, because we really aren't thinking they are watching. There able to sometimes see us without restrictions or feelings as to how we're being perceived.

We don't always give thought to how others outside of our circles perceive us and we're less inclined to go out of our way or the extra mile to say something nice. These are the areas that we want to be more attentive to we are an extension of God in the earth. Our circle knows us and most likely knows God, but those that we pass by everyday that we don't know are the people that we need to make sure that we are showing Christ to on a daily basis.

Are there people that you interact with daily that your brief interactions are not always pleasant? Maybe there's a person that's not easy to get along with. This is where you can press pause ahead of time so that the next time you interact with this person you'll be able to show the love of Christ to them. What if you decided that you would not be offended by what they do or say today? What if you choose to not take their bad attitude to heart? What if instead you take it to Christ and still show them love?

Be aware of how you interact with the people that simply pass by your life. Take a few minutes to get to know them or give them a kind word. How do you think that would change your dynamic in dealing with them?

Maybe the person you pass by isn't a problem person. Maybe you see them every week in the grocery store or doctor's office, but yet you never rise above that hand gesture or slight smile. What if, by inviting them to church the next time you see them, you change their lives?

The press pause lifestyle is all about looking at things from a broader perspective and focusing on a Kingdom Impact. Allow God to shine on areas that we can help others in. There are people that we've overlooked that we can actually have a good impact on. Maybe there are people around us that look up to us and we don't really even realize it, that we could help show the love of Christ to by letting him lead and point out those people in our paths.

Name three people that you pass throughout the month on a consistent basis that you can give a word of encouragement to:

____

____

____

Take the necessary steps to make time to encourage the three people you chose.

Find out something new about them the next time you see them.

Invite them to church with you.

⇨**Fast-forward:** Father, help me to slow down and not overlook the people that I interact with that may not be a personal friend of mine. Help me to find ways to give a smile, encouraging word, and share the love of Christ with them. Help me in the areas concerning my character that have had an effect on how I view the people I see. Go before me and light my path.

In Jesus' Name,

Amen.

PRESS PAUSE: PERCEPTIONS

Getting a new perspective is a principle that we need to help us along the way. Here were going to dig into how we look at things and how we perceive things. We will be looking into our mindsets to gain a new mindset along with our newly found perspective so be blessed let's move forward.

DAY FIFTEEN

PRESS PAUSE: HOW TO GET A NEW PERSPECTIVE

"So here's what I want you to do, God helping you: Take your everyday, ordinary life—your sleeping, eating, going-to-work, and walking-around life—and place it before God as an offering. Embracing what God does for you is the best thing you can do for him. Don't become so well-adjusted to your culture that you fit into it without even thinking. Instead, fix your attention on God. You'll be changed from the inside out. Readily recognize what he wants from you, and quickly respond to it. Unlike the culture around you, always dragging you down to its level of immaturity, God brings the best out of you, develops well-formed maturity in you." Romans 12:2 MSG

Press Pause: How do we get a new perspective? Now that we've gotten through how to press pause with God personally and in and through our relationships, it's time to get a new perspective. You have learned over the last fourteen days that despite what is going on around us, we have a choice in how we operate with God. We also have a choice of how we respond and how we choose to move throughout our days and walk through life. As we move forward, we get a new perspective by grabbing hold of the things that God has revealed and we walk them out day by day.

We can compare what we feel to the reality of where we want to be. We have to determine that we will embrace and run with our new outlook on life *(new meaning: now come in into the knowledge of)*. We can see how in the past we've looked at people, places, things, situations and experiences and allowed them dictate our lives.

As we walk out the press pause lifestyle, we now make a choice to no longer look at the problems and situations only from the natural. We will not blame people or circumstances and we will not operate unrealistically. As men and woman of God, we will take this new outlook of seeing things from the heart of God and controlling only what we can control when dealing with the things that come up in our lives. We will take this new knowledge and continually apply it to our press pause lifestyle.

This is not a pre-destined journey. The more you embrace this mindset the greater you will see your life change. Today I encourage you to fully receive God's perception for your life and walk boldly in his direction.

Thoughts & Reflections:

⇨**Fast forward:** Father I place my life and all that I am before you. Give me a new perspective and the right way to look at myself. Help me daily to walk out your way of doing things. Take out the things from this culture in me that overshadows your will and direction for my life.

In Jesus' name,

Amen.

DAY SIXTEEN

PRESS PAUSE: HOW TO GET A NEW PERSPECTIVE, PT 2

"So here's what I want you to do, God helping you: Take your everyday, ordinary life—your sleeping, eating, going-to-work, and walking-around life—and place it before God as an offering. Embracing what God does for you is the best thing you can do for him. Don't become so well-adjusted to your culture that you fit into it without even thinking. Instead, fix your attention on God. You'll be changed from the inside out. Readily recognize what he wants from you, and quickly respond to it. Unlike the culture around you, always dragging you down to its level of immaturity, God brings the best out of." Romans 12:2 MSG

In what areas are you making the choice to move forward in this new outlook of life?

Now that we're learned what we need to do to get a new perspective it's time to move in it, call it forth. We need to let God know that we're open to receive this new perspective and that we are thankful because he's allowing us to see from his eyes. Not only do we want a new perspective of looking at situations, we want a new perspective of looking at others along with our feelings, emotions, habits, and hang-ups. We don't want to stop there, we're moving forward with a new perspective of ourselves!

We want this new outlook to affect every aspect of us, all the way down to how we see and perceive ourselves. We want how we view ourselves spiritually, mentally, and physically to radically change our situation, mindset, understanding, and our beliefs of who we are and what God desires and promises to us. And when we set our heart to God, he will take us places we've never dreamed of going.

(| |)Press Pause: It's time to move forward with our new mindset and our new outlook on life. Today let's spend time in prayer with God so he can move us forward spiritually, mentally and physically in our new way of thinking and dealing with life. You have chosen to take this opportunity that many aren't willing take or don't know how to take it. You've chosen to not limit yourself in life. You are not limited by what you see or how you move and live throughout your Christian walk.

Gaining a new perspective means the old things are gone and now new things have begun. This is a celebration time! A time to think God for allowing you the understanding and desire to want to change and want something different for your life. Let's spend today celebrating and thanking God for all that he's done, everything that he's doing, and everything he is going to do in our lives.

Jot down at least three new things that you want to gain from this new perspective.

____

____

____

____

____

____

____

____

____

Pray over them ask God to lead you and direct you to what you need to do to get there and believe that he will do it. Have faith and congratulations on this new perspective.

⇨ **Fast-forward:** Heavenly father thank you for giving me the tools I need to make this new outlook on life something that I can embrace to and run with it. Thank you for blessing me with the understanding that this is something I need to do and am equipped to do.

In Jesus' name,

Amen.

DAY SEVENTEEN

PRESS PAUSE: REPROGRAMMING YOUR MIND

"But that's no life for you. You learned Christ! My assumption is that you have paid careful attention to him, been well instructed in the truth precisely as we have it in Jesus. Since, then, we do not have the excuse of ignorance, everything—and I do mean everything—connected with that old way of life has to go. It's rotten through and through. Get rid of it! And then take on an entirely new way of life—a God-fashioned life, a life renewed from the inside and working itself into your conduct as God accurately reproduces his character in you." Ephesians 4:21-24 MSG

Now it's time to look at our thinking. Over time we've learn to think wrong, ungodly, unhealthy thoughts. We've learned most of this for our peers, parents, relatives, TV, music, and videos. Many of the ungodly habits are formed because we are blind to how to think correctly. Our thoughts should be transformed to Christ thoughts and our will should line up to his will.

▶**Press Play:** Let me give you an example. A woman, we'll call her Sara, cooked her food for her family that was high in saturated fat, fried in butter or lard, and her kids learned how to eat and cook like that. This was what they learned so they repeated the cooking and eating habits. When you look at it on the surface this is a woman feeding her family, but as you look at it holistically, Sara is creating bad habits that could destroy the lives of the children she loves.

Sara can't help it. It's all she knows and it's all her children know, unless they get exposed to the truth. The only way for Sara to change her way of cooking is to get a new perspective on food and then change her mindset about how she should cook. Sara has to realize that there's something else out there and be introduced to something new. That's the only way she can embrace a new healthier way.

Likewise our parents, peers and even teachers program our thoughts. If someone of influence or authority said and confessed things like " I'm broke. You're no good. You won't succeed," you can begin to think that those things are true.

That's why it critical to hear what God has to say about us and accept those words of life as truth in our lives.

(| |)Press Pause: Your thought patterns may not align with the word of God right now. It's okay and it's not your fault, but you are about to be faced with truth. If what you think doesn't align with the word of God, now is the time for a mindset makeover, which can only be done through the word of God.

When accepting this new mindset, it's your responsibility to change the way you think. The great thing about being a Christian is that Christ has given us a way to do this. The best way for you to change your thought patterns is to get into a Bible preaching and teaching church, attend every Sunday morning service and actively study what you are learning. The Bible says faith comes by hearing and hearing the word of God. You can also change your mindset through pressing pause and understanding the root of your actions, thoughts and words.

Who has had the most influence over your life throughout the years?

____

____

____

Who have you let influence your thoughts that you should not have let have so much influence over your thinking?

____

____

____

What is one media outlet that has been influential on your thoughts?

____

____

____

What are three steps that you can take to stop the influential people and or media outlets from impacting your mindset?

____
____
____

Pinpoint at least one area in your thinking that will help bring you the most change.

____
____
____

Thoughts & Reflections:

⇨**Fast forward**: Father I realize that there are areas within my thought life that I have neglected. I ask that as I get quiet with you that you would show me the areas in my mindset that are unbalanced and wrong. I thank you father that as you show me these my mindset will change. Thank you for your love, comfort, kindness, and support as you provide clarity in who you are and all that you want me to be.

In Jesus' Name,

Amen.

DAY EIGHTEEN

PRESS PAUSE: PRESS PAUSE REPROGRAMMING YOUR MIND, PT 2

"But that's no life for you. You learned Christ! My assumption is that you have paid careful attention to him, been well instructed in the truth precisely as we have it in Jesus. Since, then, we do not have the excuse of ignorance, everything—and I do mean everything—connected with that old way of life has to go. It's rotten through and through. Get rid of it! And then take on an entirely new way of life—a God-fashioned life, a life renewed from the inside and working itself into your conduct as God accurately reproduces his character in you." Ephesians 4:21-24 MSG

Now that we've pinpointed some of the areas, people, places, and outlets that have had an effect on our thoughts and our way of thinking, it's time for us to dig into what it takes to reprogram our way of thinking. Reprogramming our mind is not something that is going to come easy, because you already have so much in there to go back and change. Your thought patterns, mindset and even your understanding on how you process things and situations will need to be reprogrammed. This part is going to take a little extra effort to really combat your thoughts, because at times you will feel like you're in all-out war with your mind. As they come up, let go of things that you have always believed to be true and agree to see them from God's new perspective. Reprogram your different thought processes by digging into the things that God has illuminated through the journey no matter how uncomfortable or un-Orthodox it may feel. Be willing and ready to press through, reprogram, and realign your mind with godly thinking and Biblical mindset.

(| |) Press Pause: When you're patterns and thoughts come up, how do you combat? Here are a few beneficial keys that will help you fight against the old ways of thinking. When a thought comes to your mind or you find yourself ready to operate in an old pattern, immediately cast it out your mind by replacing it with God's word. When you find yourself falling into the same old actions, quote scriptures that will help you focus in the direction that you want to go. Get into your word daily and continue to sit with God. Ask him for his help to stay on track. If you fall off, know that you can get up and try again. God will help you to think his thoughts, walk in a clearer path, and lead you along the way. Simply open your heart to the change.

Find at least three Scriptures in the Bible that deals with a new way of godly thinking.

____

____

____

Write those Scriptures out on index cards and keep them in your wallet or pocketbook.

Say those scriptures at least twice a day and meditate on them (ponder, think, reflect) throughout your day.

When your old ways of thinking and doing things come up in your mind tell yourself you no longer have to think those thoughts or do those things. Don't be afraid to talk to yourself. Look in the mirror and declare, "I'm becoming my best version of me, because I am transforming into all that God designed me to be."

⇨**Fast forward:** Father, I thank you that you are always here for me, father I thank you for your living word that always speaks life over me. I ask that you help me to go the distance in this journey of changing my mind, thinking, and they way that I operate. I ask that you help me weed out the wrong influences in my life so that they no longer take root in my mind. Put new seeds of healthy thinking and actions and set me around influential people who help me succeed.

In Jesus' name,

Amen.

PRESS PAUSE: REFLECTING ON GOD

This where you experience an intimate encounter with God. Here it's all about God, who he is, who he wants to be, and what he can be for you. Make sure as you're reflecting on yourself and your relationships, that we know who God wants to be in your life. Nurture your intimate relationship with God. As you're doing this, set in our hearts that you are loved by God.

Remember, God is for you no matter where you find yourself in your Christian walk. As you walk through this portion of the journey, let him love on you, let his words speak to you while you meditate and reflect on him. Move forward and let God download more of his spirit and love on you.

DAY NINETEEN
PRESS PAUSE: GOD CARES

"So be content with who you are, and don't put on airs. God's strong hand is on you; he'll promote you at the right time. Live carefree before God; he is most careful with you."
1 Peter 5:7

Who is God to you? No matter who he has been to in the past, if he's been this distant being or a faraway father, I want you to know now that he is your God. So many times in the past we may have seen God as the Lord of our lives, but not as someone that's concerned with our day-to-day dealings. That is so far from the truth. God, the one and only true living God, is close at all times and he wants to be a part of our everyday life. God cares for us and is just as concerned with the things that are on our minds and in our hearts as we are. Truthfully he's more concerned and that's why he tries so hard to guide us through this life because he wants the best for us. He doesn't want better for us, he wants the absolute best for us in every area of our lives.

God is not this puppet ruler that made a

world just so he can control it. Cast those things out of your head, because that is not God. God is our heavenly father and he loves us as his children. And as we continue to get this picture of our father God in our mind, the more he can and will reveal himself to us.

God has many names and he has them for a reason. Each name shares of God's attributes. His names hold a certain outcome and a purpose. As we reflect on God and who he is for us, we must make sure we're open and willing to hear who he is. Let's not hear or take in what others are saying or feeling, but be in tune to God. Let him show us who he is in our lives.

(||)Press Pause: Let's make sure were getting all of the outside distractions and noises from our heart and minds to focus totally on God. Let his word and who he tells us he is and wants to be to us personally. He wants to be so much more than what he has been for us in the past. It's safe to say that he wants to be our everything; he wants to be our first love, our first thought, the first that we run to, the first that we seek, and the first that we desire.

Do you really believe that God cares about you and your daily concerns?

____

What areas in your life can you identify that God cares for you?

____

____

____

____

____

____

In what areas do you feel you need help in seeing God as a loving and caring father for your life?

____

____

____

Find two Scriptures in the Bible about God's love for you and how he sees you.

Write out those Scriptures and tape them to your bathroom mirror. Read them aloud each morning.

⇨**Fast-forward:** Father, allow me to see you for who you are in every area of my life. Thank you for being willing to reveal yourself to me. I ask that as I continue to draw closer to you and as I continue to seek you, that you will continually reveal yourself to me through dreams, visions, and your word.

I pray that I would get to know your will for my life. I thank you that you want the best for me and are concerned with the things that concern me and my sphere of influence. Father you already see me full and whole, let me see myself as you see me.

In Jesus' name,

Amen.

DAY TWENTY

PRESS PAUSE: GOD LOVE

"We cannot round up enough containers to hold everything God generously pours into our lives through the Holy spirit! Christ arrives right on time to make this happen. He didn't, and doesn't, wait for us to get ready. He presented himself for his sacrificial death when we were far too weak in rebellious to do anything to get ourselves ready. And even if we hadn't been so weak, we wouldn't have known what to do anyway. We can understand someone dying for a person worth dying for, and we can understand how someone good and noble could inspire us to selfless sacrifice. But God put his love on the line for us by offering his son in sacrificial death while we were of no use whatsoever to him. Now that we are set right with God by means of the sacrificial death, the consummate blood sacrifice, there is no longer a question of being at odds with God in any way. If, when we were at our worst, we were put on friendly terms with God by the sacrificial death of his son, now that we're at our best, just thinking of how our lives will expand and deepen by means of his resurrection life! Now that we

have actually received this amazing friendship with God, we are no longer content to simply say it in parlaying poise we sing and shout out praises to God through Jesus, the Messiah!"
Romans 5:5-11

God is love and love is his nature. We are special to him. God doesn't love us because of all the good we've done or because of how perfect we are, he loves us because he IS love.

▶**Press Play:** Glory to your name! You are so awesome father God and your love for us is so amazing. Not only do you love us, but the way you love us is even more incredible. You love us in a way that's unfathomable for words. God does not just love us because of the good we do, he loves us because of who he is and who he sees we are.

God see the good in us even when we are not able to it see it in ourselves. God sees us as whole and not as our past or our mistakes. He chooses to love us in spite of our faults, our past, our downfalls, or our attitudes.

He chooses us when we were not willing to choose ourselves and showered his untainted, unhindered, everlasting never ceasing love on us.

We must realize how valuable we are to him. Know that you are appreciated, one-off-a-kind, loved, special treasure to God. Let's make sure that we receive love from God and that we reflect on it.

We have to receive love especially the love from God, which will give us the strength and foundation we need to give love to others.

(||)Press Pause: Once we open our mind, our heart, and our attitude to receive and accept the love of God, we position ourselves to in return be able to truly love others. This is vital to experiencing an abundant life in God. Once we learn that God loves us and how to love ourselves, this sets us on a platform to be able to receive the more abundant and extravagant life in God. We place ourselves in a position to bring joy in our lives because we know we're loved. We know that we're filled in that area.

Now I know that, because of the way God loves me. He showed me how to love myself by giving me this opportunity to sit down and communion with him about me. I now can receive the joy that he wants to bring, the peace, the hope and the blessings that he wants for my life. My eyes are open because the more I know who God is, the more I'll begin to understand how he wants to and delights in my prosperity. This is not just prospering financially, but emotionally, physically, mentally and spiritually.

God wants to love us to shower his love upon us and to shower us with his anointing, his blessing, his prosperity and his favor. Remember this, our God is a great God and he wants to show us and give us a greater way of living, living a life of freedom from guilt and condemnation.

Meditate on the Scripture above all day today and ask God that as you meditate on it to shower and surround you in his love.

Thoughts & Reflections:

⇨**Fast Forward:** Father, I thank you for seeing me and choosing me when I wasn't able to see or choose myself. Father I thank you for your love and for your kindness and mercies that are renewed every morning. I thank you that you love me more than I could ever know. I ask that as you love on me, give me the strength, will and determination to let your love flow freely from me to others. I love you, I cherish you, and I receive your love for me.

In Jesus' name,

Amen.

DAY TWENTY-ONE
PRESS PAUSE: THE CROSS

*"Then the angel spoke to the women. "Don't be afraid!" he said. "I know you are looking for Jesus, who was crucified. **6** He isn't here! He is risen from the dead, just as he said would happen. Come, see where his body was lying."*

Matthew 28:5-6 KJV

Imagine a time when violent and oppressive pagans overtake your country. This is what it was like during the time when Jesus was born. The Jews during the life of Jesus were looking for a Messiah to rescue them from Rome. They were oppressed by Roman commanders, paganism, and by Roman violence. The Jews were looking for the Messiah to be a military commander, lead them to victory and out of their oppression. When Jesus came he brought the good news, healing the sick and blind, and allowing the lame to walk. Even though Jesus came and brought healing to thousands, the Jews were not able to recognize him as the Messiah.

Despite all of his mighty works, they weren't looking for a Messiah to come as a lamb and

Jesus was rejected. Jesus' rejections led him to be traded by one of his disciples, tortured, and put on the cross. When this happened to him it allowed his believers the ability to be changed. We were saved, set free and able to inherit all of heaven's riches through his sacrifice.

(| |) Press Pause: As a follower of Christ you will be rejected at times. Even though rejection will happen, Jesus teaches us to rejoice when people say or do bad things, because we are his followers. It may seem somewhat bizarre, but it really isn't. The Bible teaches us that things won't always be easy. The cross was never an easy thing for Christ to do, but he did it. He allowed the sins of this world to fall up on his shoulders and just thinking about that, it couldn't have been in no way shape or form a pleasant burden to carry.

Not only does the cross and what Jesus did for us show that rejection would come, it also shows us that with him we can move forward with joy and peace when facing our own crosses. Knowing that Christ died on the cross by laying down his life and then return victorious with all power in his hands we see the power even in suffering. Because of Christ, we are victorious all the time.

Even though some did not see our Savior as the Messiah he was, the cross shows us so many different perspectives of God, as well as his power and glory that would be too vast to tell in one setting. What we can see is that we ourselves may not always come wrapped in a shining packet that is likable and loved by everyone, but when we come to our Messiah, he sees us as beautiful and glorious.

He is willing to walk alongside us, before us, and behind us to ensure our safety and victory in our Christian walk. God is more than able to bring us out victorious every time. We may not always see the victory. Sometimes we may have to squint our eyes, but we have to know that God is always working things out for our good. Stand tall knowing that we are covered. Not only are we covered in victory, but the cross has also covered ALL our sins.

Have you ever had to deal with being rejected?

____

____

____

How did you learn to deal with or get over rejection?

____

____

____

____

____

____

Name two ways you can see God's love for you as you reflect on the things that he's done for you in regards to the cross?

____

____

____

Find two Scriptures to help you in times of rejection that you can reflect on to get strength, healing and the ability to look to God during those time.

Thoughts & Reflections:

⇨**Fast forward:** Father I thank you from the bottom of my heart for sending your son Jesus to take all of our sins and allow us a chance to be with you. Thank you Jesus for becoming the bridge that we needed to have a greater life. Thank you for going through so much just for us.

In Jesus' name,

Amen.

DAY TWENTY-TWO
PRESS PAUSE: FORGIVENESS THROUGH GOD

All that passing laws against sin did was produce more lawbreakers. But sin didn't, and doesn't, have a chance in competition with the aggressive forgiveness we call grace. When it's sin versus grace, grace wins hands down. All sin can do is threaten us with death, and that's the end of it. Grace, because God is putting everything together again through the Messiah, invites us into life—a life that goes on and on and on, world without end.

Romans 5:20-21 MSG

▶**Press Play:** When think about forgiveness one of many stories sticks out to me more so than others. After Jesus, the Jews still had problems with Christians. There was a Pharisee among Pharisees named Saul who was so focused on stamping out Christianity that he would get papers from the high priest to have Christian stoned and arrested. One day on his way to Damascus, where he was going to persecute Christians, Christ appeared to him and said, “Saul, Saul why do you persecute me?” This is the beginning of Saul’s conversion.

After Christ appeared to Saul he was blind for three days. He was sent to a believers house name Ananias, who prayed for him and he received his vision back. God told Ananias that Saul would be an instrument of his to carry God’s name before the Gentiles from that day forward. Saul who was later called Paul, preached the gospel and became one of the most influential early church planters and evangelists.

(| |) Press Pause: Even though Paul had been a Christian killer in his former life, Jesus was able to forgive him and use him for a new work. No matter what you’ve done or where you’ve come from, Christ is able to forgive you and use you. God’s love manifests in a forgiving power that reaches beyond our understanding. Know this, no matter what’s in your past or what you’re doing in the present, our God is able and willing to forgive you and set you on Straight Street if you will believe.

Wherever you find yourself in our Christian walk just remember you are forgiven through God.

Today take time to thank God for forgiving you from you past and sins, ask him to help you stand strong on his word and trust in him.

Thoughts & Reflections:

⇨**Fast forward:** Father thank you for being a forgiving God. Thank you for loving us enough to wash us clean and make us in your image. Help me to be mindful at all times of your kindness and help me show that same kindness to others. I love you.

In Jesus' name,

Amen.

DAY TWENTY-THREE

PRESS PAUSE: REFLECTING ON GOD'S GRACE

"His son said to him, 'Father, I have sinned against both heaven and you, and I am no longer worthy of being called your son." But his father said to the servants, 'Quick! Bring the finest robe in the house and put it on him. Get a ring for his finger and sandals for his feet. And kill the calf we have been fattening. We must celebrate with a feast, for this son of mine was dead and has now returned to life. He was lost, but now he is found. So the party began."

Luke 15:21-24 MSG

Sin is a subject that people don't always want to talk about, sin is what separates us from God and is what damages the people we love the most. It also hurts us and it's how we hurt ourselves. The wages of sin is death and all who sin fall short of the glory of God. When you sin, you are separating yourself from God in your earning death. Now we all will die, but that doesn't mean we need or have to go to hell, which is the second death.

Even though we earned it, we have a great helper. God's grace is sufficient to give us eternal life. God's will is that no man goes to hell. His will is that we all spend eternity with him in heaven. Through his grace, his willingness to give us something we don't deserve along with the sacrifices of Jesus Christ allows us to get in heaven. It's a gift. His grace is sufficient to meet our needs in this life and in the next.

(| |) Press Pause: Have you ever had a child act up the day before their birthday or the day before Christmas? As a parent you wanted to discipline them or you thought about holding back their present, right? Although you want to, usually something in us simply can't deny them of that gift, even after wrongdoing. Just imagine how God feels after we let him down over and over and over again.

Before we were saved we looked for opportunities to sin. We were living a lifestyle that was not right with him. We didn't even understand that what we were doing was separating us from God. Once we got saved and accepted Jesus Christ as our Lord, God's grace was given to us.

Now just like a child who is acting up the day before Christmas or the day before their birthday, you still get to keep your present. In everything that we do, let's make an effort to allow Gods grace to keep us close to him.

Today let's reflect on God's grace and get in his word on today.

____

____

____

____

____

____

____

____

____

____

____

____

⇨**Fast forward:** God your grace is enough for me. I take this time to thank you for it and for all the blessings that come along with it. Help me to stay close to you and not do anything that would separate me from you.

In Jesus' name,

Amen.

JUMPSTART YOUR PRESS PAUSE LIFESTYLE

DECLARATIONS AND ACTIVATIONS

Pat yourself on the back you made it to the final stretch of this thirty-day. Press Pause life changing journey. Now it's time to start speaking this press pause lifestyle into existence. Over the next few days I'm going to give you keys and insight that will jumpstart your newly found lifestyle. So let's get ready set go we are approaching the finish line.

DAY TWENTY-FOUR

PRESS PAUSE DAILY

"Study to shew thyself approved unto God, a workman that needeth not to be ashamed, rightly dividing the word of truth."
2 Timothy 2:15 KJV

Now it's time for us press pause daily beyond the thirty-day journey. Plan to do this every day so you can have a great year. Look at your current daily schedule and the time you get up in the morning so that you can create your Morning Pause. Maybe it's the same time as your already getting up to do your devotional.

What time would you have to get up in order to incorporate your **Morning Pause** each day?

____

How long do you plan to take out of your day for your **Morning Pause?**

5 minutes 10 minutes 15 minutes

20 minutes 30 minutes 45 minutes

You need your Bible to get into the word, study scriptures, and make sure that its getting down in your heart. God's word is like our instruction manual and a daily guiding light for us. Continue to journal this during this time and don't be afraid to highlight the scriptures that really speak to your heart. Make sure you take out time to reflect and meditate on a scripture and watch how God continues to work in your life.

⇨**Fast forward:** God help me to make time for you in my everyday life. As I spend time with you, reveal yourself to me. Show me how to walk with you and in your word.

In Jesus' name,

Amen.

DAY TWENTY-FIVE
PRESS PAUSE BEFORE RESPONDING

"A gentle response defuses anger, but a sharp tongue kindles a temper-fire."

Proverbs 15:1 KJV

Are you ready to incorporate this press pause lifestyle into your life? Well I hope so, because today we're going to journal ways that will help us moving forward in our newly found way of life. Grab your journal, highlighter, pen or pencil and of course you're Bible.

▶**Press Play:** It's important that we get a game plan ahead of time on ways that we can operate our lives to be better prepared for those press pause moments. One of the ways we'll do it is by finding at least three response practices that we are able to adopt that fits our lifestyle and personality.

Then we'll practice them out, yes were going to actually practice some of our responses out ahead of time. Why are we doing this you ask, because it helps develop a good habit of responding rightly and thinking about our response and reactions in the heat of a difficult time. Just like with reading the word daily, the more you're feeding yourself with understanding the press pause lifestyle, the more apt you are to use what you read when faced with opposition.

If I'm continually feeding myself the word when something comes up, I'll be quick to give it to God, reflect on his word and response in a manner that pleases God.

(| |) Press Pause: I'm going to give you some of my top response suggestions and I want you to look through each one thoroughly. See if it's something that you can see yourself doing. Now while you don't have to choose all of them, you do have to decide to start practicing three of them to move forward and incorporate into your daily life.

1. When dealing and thinking about conflict, let us first remember that we are representing Christ first and foremost. We want to always keep that in our mind and hearts when we address situations.

2. We are a reflection of Christ, so even if we're not directly doing or in something,

our being there or not standing up for righteousness can be misrepresented and misunderstood. We have to really be aware of the things we do, say, and how we act or not act on things as well.

3. At the first sign of you feeling upset from a situation, press pause and gather yourself, pray for help, receive peace and expect God to step in. If possible and within reason, peacefully try to diffuse the situation. If not possible politely and gracefully excuse yourself. If it's something going on that you need to stand your ground in then do so with your character in mind. Everything is not always something that you can walk away from. There are times that you may have to be firm on things and in that its ok to rightfully stand your ground.

4. If you walk into a situation unknowingly and something or someone comes up abruptly and you weren't able to see it ahead of time, you have to deal with it. Take a deep breath, don't respond initially, press pause in your response. Be polite and as nice as possible. Try to help

if it concerns you, but if it isn't addressed to you then don't opt in.

5. If throughout your day, you feel yourself uneasy or emotional for whatever reason or you feel that you're off-balance, take ten minutes find yourself a quiet place to press pause. Reflect on God and his word. Ask him to give you peace and the patience you need to go about your day.

6. If you had an emotional conversation or incident with someone close to you, say a friend or family member and you're feeling hurt or unfairly treated, take a press pause moment reflect on God. Try to separate your emotions from what happened and look into what you're really feeling. Are they relevant feelings from just this situation or are there remnants of past feelings that you still need to deal with? Once you evaluate those things, ask God to step in and begin to heal you so you can be set free from letting your emotions get the best of you. Take time out, this press pause may need to be for a day or two to get healed. Let any bitterness and angry feelings go. Give

them to God and ask him to let you know the right time to go back and reconcile the situation.

7. No matter what has gone on or what has happened make sure that you leave it there. Try to compartmentalize what happen and don't take it with you. If you're at work don't bring it home and if it's from home don't bring it to work with you. Process it and deal with it at the right time in the right and appropriate place.

   Remember you have to be intentional to keep your character and your integrity intact. You have all rights to live a peaceful, happy and whole life and what we learned during this time is that you don't have to be moved or blown in the wind just because somebody else wants to try and toss you around.
8. Now the last scenario it could be a little touchier because it deals with family, loved ones, or people that we hold close to her heart. Those are the times when hurt is involved. In feelings of wrongdoing or wrongful treatment, we do have to press

pause and give it to God, because we do know and love those people. We do have to go back to reconcile, but in the right time. Ask God to help you heal, that way you're not relying on a solution from the other person to move forward. Give it to God. Let God heal you and move along.

⇨**Fast forward:** Father, I appreciate all that you have taught me and are continuing to teach me every day. I ask that you would go before me and help me to respond with right actions when I respond to people. I am trying to continually live right before you, to be more like you and to respond, as you would have me. Because I was made in your image, I want to be a great reflection of who you are. Let me take advantage of my press pause moments as I move throughout my day.

In Jesus name,

Amen.

A Note of Knowledge: *So then my beloved brethren, let every man be swift to hear, slow to speak, slow to wrath; for the wrath of man does not produce the righteousness of God. James 1:9*

DAY TWENTY-SIX

PRESS PAUSE IN THE WORD

"And here's why: GOD gives out Wisdom free, is plainspoken in Knowledge and Understanding. He's a rich man of Common Sense for those who live well, a personal bodyguard to the candid and sincere. He keeps his eye on all who live honestly, and pays special attention to his loyally committed ones."
Proverbs 2:6 MSG

It is important to get into the word of God every day, so let's find the way that is best for you to be able to do that. One thing that I know is that we need to have a plan of action because things can come up through our day that can distract us and take us away from getting in our word. One of the best ways to combat this is to plan it out. Today work on the plan of action, but know that the time can change. All that matters is that we try to do it.

How many minutes a day can you set aside to spend time in your word?

What will you commit to reading a scripture passage or will you commit to a chapter?

There is no right or wrong way it just depends on the time that you have.

▶**Press Play:** Make sure you use a Bible that you can understand easily. For a lot of people, the King James is not easily understood. I suggest the NIV, NIV study Bible, the Amplified Bible or the New Living Bible. You can choose these or look for your own. It's also okay to have more than one kind in your home library, because you can always read in multiple versions.

(| |) Press Pause: Take the time to commit to a reading schedule. The time may have to be adjusted based on your schedule or during life changes, but be faithful to have your time in God's word. Life in the word will give you so much power and energy to change your day, your week, your year and your life. Go forth and be blessed. Emerge yourself in the word of God.

Side Note: If you're not sure where you want to start I always like to suggest that you start with the basics. Start your Bible reading with the Gospels; Matthew, Mark, Luke, and John which are found in the New Testament.

Today let's start with getting to know Jesus. It's truly amazing that no matter how long you've been with the Lord, there are new things you will discover when you read the bible.

God is always showing you something in a different way than before. It's like a new life lesson when you open the Bible. Getting back to the basic' is a great place to start today, so let's read and meditate on Matt 18.

Thoughts & Reflections:

DAY TWENTY-SEVEN
PRESS PAUSE MEDITATIONS

"...And don't for a minute let this Book of The Revelation be out of mind. Ponder and meditate on it day and night, making sure you practice everything written in it. Then you'll get where you're going; then you'll succeed. Haven't I commanded you? Strength! Courage! Don't be timid; don't get discouraged. God, *your God, is with you every step you take."*

Joshua 1:8 MSG

What does it mean to meditate? Meditation is to go over and spend time thinking on the word or a word from God. Think about that one passage or word throughout your day. Ask for understanding of it, rehearse it and recite the word in your mind or out loud. The key is to get it down in your heart.

For my words have I hid in your heart so that you might not sin against me.

My words is a lamp unto your feet, and a light on to your path.

Meditate on my word both day and night.

▶**Press Play:** Today we're going to get into different scriptures that we can meditate on throughout the day. They are separated by the overall theme so that you are able to find the subject and meditate on that subject throughout your day. You don't have to find or look up every Scripture or meditate on every subject that is on the list. Simply choose a subject and at least one or two scriptures from that subject to meditate on.

Take this time to look in your journal and see if there was a subject throughout this journey that really stood out for you, meditate on that for today.

Example of meditation:

"Strong God, I'm watching you do it,
I can always count on you—
God, my dependable love."

Psalms 59:17

Throughout the day you repeat this passage over to yourself. You can also put yourself in it. "God thank you for watching over me and being my strong tower. God I'm glad that I can always depend on you and that you always love me." As you do this, pray and talk to God during your day. Keep going over it until its down in your heart.

(| |) **Press Pause**: Now it's time to get started, make sure you have your journal and get ready to meditate and reflect on God's word. As you're reading and reflecting on God's word, ask him to highlight areas that will help you on your journey.

Relationships

New Testament

Matthew 7:12, Luke 6:37 – 38, *Romans 12:9 – 18, 2Corinthians 5:16 – 18, Galatians 6:1 – 5, Philippians 2:1 – 4, Titus 3:7, 3 John 5

Love

The Old Testament

Psalms 59:17, Proverbs 15:17; Proverbs 20:6

The New Testament

Matthew 22:37 – 40, John 12:25; John 15:19, *Romans 5:8, Romans 8:35, Ephesians 3:17 – 19, Ephesians 5:1 – 2, 1

John 2:15

Happiness

The Old Testament

Psalms 16:8 – 9, Psalms 103:5, Psalms 119:111, Proverbs 13:7

New Testament

Romans 12:15, Philippians 4:4, Philippians 4:12

Health

Old Testament

Proverbs 17:22

New Testament

Luke 6:44, 1 Corinthians 12:24, 1Corinthians 12:25- 28, 1Timothy 4:8 – 9, James 5:13 – 16, 1 Peter 2:24

DAY TWENTY-EIGHT

PRESS PAUSE DECLARATION

Today is the day of declarations and as we do these, I want you to believe by faith that you can have what God says you can have, that you are who God says you are, and that you can be all that God says you can be. Take off your seatbelt, stand boldly and declare these declarations these words over your life. Say them with boldness, faith, enthusiasm, joy and a smile.

ARE YOU READY!!!

▶**Press Play:** This is the day that the Lord has made, I make a choice to be glad in it.

I choose to walk love

I choose to operate in peace

I choose joy

I am full of hope

I am surrounded by peace

I am new in Christ

I am determined

I have wealth

I have wisdom

I walk in grace

I have self-control

I am focused

I am made whole through Christ

I've been forgiven of all my sins

I have knowledge

I'm a good person

I am the righteousness of God through Christ Jesus

My body is the temple of the Holy Spirit

I've been freed from condemnation

I am a saint

I am called of God

I have vision

I have direction

I have dreams

I am fearfully and wonderfully made

I am the head and not the tail

I am above and not beneath

I am the first and never the last

I've been chosen by God

I am holy and blameless before God

I'm blessed in my relationships

I'm blessed physically

I'm blessed mentally

My feelings are blessed

My emotions are blessed

My body is blessed

I'm blessed in the city

I'm blessed in the field

I'm blessed when I come

I'm blessed when I go

Greater is he that is in me then he that's in the world

I am more than a conqueror

My finances are blessed

I believe God for dreams

I believe God for vision

I believe God for opportunities on my job

I believe God for bonuses and raises

I'm believe God for favor everywhere I go

(| |) Press Pause: I am so happy that we've made it to this day. Make copies of these declarations post them in places that you frequent around your house. Post on your bathroom mirror, in the kitchen where you can see it when you're cooking, in the living room and anywhere else that you may need to press pause at throughout your day.

There is no magic amount of times that you should do these declarations. Don't limit yourself. Anytime you need them, whip them out and start speaking over your life. A good starting point would be at least three times a day. The more you do them, you'll start to memorize them and start adding to them. They'll begin to flow naturally.

Thoughts & Reflections:

⇨**Fast-forward:** God, I thank you that today is a new day. Thank you for my new outlook on life. I'm ready to speak my new life in you into existence. I will declare and decree your will for me and because I do so, I will live in the land of more than enough. I declare that my home and family overflow. Our needs are met and we have enough left over to help other and advance the kingdom of God. Thank you for filling my mouth with your words.

In the mighty name of Jesus,

Amen.

DAY TWENTY-NINE

PRESS PAUSE: USE YOUR TONGUE

"With the tongue we praise our Lord and Father, and with it we curse human beings, who have been made in God's likeness. Out of the same mouth come praise and cursing. My brothers and sisters, this should not be. Can both fresh water and salt water flow from the same spring? My brothers and sisters, can a fig tree bear olives, or a grapevine bear figs? Neither can a salt spring produce fresh water." James 3:9-11 KVJ

▶**Press Play:** We were made in the image of God. When we look at who God is we know that he's the creator. He created the world that we live in with just his words. Because he made us in his image, he's given that creative power to us. Our words are more important than we could ever imagine.

It's time to use our tongue to exercise this awesome God-given creative power. Do not be fooled into thinking it's going to be easy, because as we're speaking, things might try to get into our head and urge us to speak against what we believe God for. Don't let fear, doubt, or unbelief get into your mind.

Make a choice that no matter what, you're going to speak by faith the word of God and expect for the good things you are speaking to happen.

Confess these out loud:

I am a new creature in Christ, the old things have passed away and behold all things are new.

I am the righteousness in God through Christ Jesus.

I am willing and wanting to spend precious time with God.

I want to get to know myself better through God my creator.

My relationships are getting better and better.

I am beginning to see myself through God's eyes.

I'm learning to love my reflection.

I value the things of God and want to be a reflection of him.

I can do all things through Christ who gives me strength.

I am of good character and integrity.

I am far from oppression.

Fear does not come near me.

I am going to live out my God-given purpose.

This will be one of the best days this far.

I am healthy.

I am whole through Christ Jesus.

I am well.

I will have a great year and be successful.

My children are blessed and doing great.

My house is in order.

My life is in order.

My family is in order.

My relationship is in order.

I will live the life I have always dream of.

I see things turning around for my good.

I'm going into a new level with God.

I believing God will show me things I need to work on.

I believe God has given me the tools to fix what is broken in my life.

I live a life healthy and free from guilt and condemnation.

(❙❙) **Press Pause**: Think of two more faith confessions that you can add to this list. Add it in your journal and post it around you personal spaces. Be intentional to say them at least once a day and journal along your journey and measure the results of this daily discipline.

⇨**Fast-forward:** Father God I thank you for being the creator of the universe. I thank you for creating me in your image and giving me the tools I need to walk in the authority that you've given me through the Word. I ask that as I speak things into existence, that I would exercise it according to your word and will for my life. Help me to be bold and fearless in my words. Let me speak a better life, health and understanding to take me into my future. I receive a new life of liberty and freedom in you.

In Jesus' name,

Amen.

DAY THIRTY

PRESS PAUSE: PRAYER & RELEASE

You made it to the finish line, which in actuality is the start line. You may be finished with this thirty-day journey, but it's the start of a new lifestyle for you. Take everything in that you learned over these days and apply them to your life. Keep the word of God in your heart and move forward in Jesus name.

God wants us to live a life of hope; peace, love, respect, thankfulness and passion for him and you can do this. You've already taken a month and dedicated it to pressing pause and reflecting on God. Now today is the day of prayer and release for your future so get your heart and mind ready to receive the abundance and the overflow that God has planned for you. Let nothing or no one separate you from the love of God. Go forth in God and trust that he will give you the strength and ability to do so.

⇨**Fast-forward:** God I thank you for this journey. I thank you for how you shed light to some dark areas in my life. Father let the people around me see the change in me, more importantly let me see the change that you have done to me. I declare that this transformation is long standing. As I move forward, let me see people through your eyes. Let me walk in faith and believe you to maximize my life.

God I thank you for this relationship that is strengthened daily as I take time with you. New levels are waiting for me and I declare that greater works you will have me do. Thank you for your peace, joy, and strength.

In Jesus' name,

Amen.

▶**Press Play:** In the name of Jesus, I release your people to run with a passion for you towards your perfect will. Let a desire to move with you consume their hearts and ignite their purpose. I declare that they are moving forward as salt and light in the earth. Give them a new zeal for life. Let them be strengthen by you.

Father God as you release them, continually give them insight and increase with their checks and balance system. As they go forth in you let them remember to press pause making sure that they are spiritually aligned to your will.

Thank you for the grace to live this lifestyle. May they relentlessly seek your face and as they do so, shower blessings on them that they couldn't even imagine. Your word says no eye has seen, ear has heard, and no mind has imagined what God has prepared. I call forth the unimaginable to manifest in their life. Supersede their wildest dreams and take them into a new season.

I send you out in the power and authority of Jesus to impact the lives of those in your sphere of influence. Walk, run and always press pause so that you may transform the lives of those around you!

Thoughts & Reflections:

DAY THIRTY-ONE

PRESS PAUSE: BONUS DAY

This is a bonus day for the months that have thirty-one days or in case you simply need a Press Pause refresher. Today is all about staying prepared as you walk into this newly found lifestyle. Make sure to journal, journal, journal and look back regularly to see your progress.

As you complete this journey, I encourage you to get a fresh journal for you to keep a continual record of you press pause moments in. This way you can see how you are handling the challenges that come your way. It will be lots of fun to read those stories months down the line and you'll be able to say, "Look what the Lord has done!" If your life is anything like mine, you'll probably have a few novels from your experiences. You can also look back and see what scriptures helped you through certain situations. You may find some patterns when it comes to go-to prescriptions for challenging moments.

(| |) **Press Pause**: Read James 1 mediate on its truth and how it resonates with your life. I'll get you started with the first passage and then you finish strong on the rest. This is your moment to show your growth in God. Let the word of God come alive today as you read. Hide this word in your heart and what ever your do...

Don't forget to press pause!

James, a servant of God and of the Lord Jesus Christ, To the twelve tribes scattered among the nations: Greetings. Trials and temptations consider it pure joy, my brothers and sisters, whenever you face trials of many kinds, because you know that the testing of your faith produces perseverance.

James 1:1-3

ABOUT THE AUTHOR

Speaker ~ Author ~ Coach

Lakisha Shaffer is a dynamic motivational speaker, coach and Bible teacher, with a passion to empower others for powerful living. As a mother, wife and entrepreneur she has created a unique way to navigate through life's challenges and it is through her own journey, she has discovered the "Press Pause" message.

www.ingramcontent.com/pod-product-compliance
Lightning Source LLC
Chambersburg PA
CBHW071336090426
42738CB00012B/2912

* 9 7 8 0 6 9 2 4 1 6 8 2 2 *